She Who Wears the Crown

Alean H. Smith

Contents

Dedication i

Acknowledgments ii

About the Author iii

Introduction 1

Part One For All the Women 9

Chapter 1: Opposition vs. Opportunity 10

Chapter 2: Focus... 22

Chapter 3: Transforming Your Mindset..................... 31

Chapter 4: The Road Less Traveled 39

Chapter 5: Matters of the Heart.................................. 52

Chapter 6: Birthing Your Gifts 68

Chapter 7: Operating In Wisdom................................. 76

Chapter 8: God's Promises 88

In Closing... 101

Nine Key Takeaways 111

Part Two For Teen Girls 112

Chapter 1: Who Am I? Discovering My Purpose! 115

Chapter 2: What Are Worth and Self-Validation? 120

Chapter 3: Overcoming Social Pressures.................... 127

Chapter 4: Just Dream 134

Wrap Up... 141

References... 146

Dedication

May this book serve as a beacon of hope and inspiration to those who have yet to uncover their purpose and to those who are already fulfilling their destiny by making a difference in the lives of others.

Acknowledgments

Before I begin this journey with you, I must take a moment and humbly give accolades to the Heavenly Father.

The Holy Spirit has guided me through this entire process with His infinite understanding of knowledge and wisdom.

This journey would not have been possible without your guidance.

You are the Master teacher, a compass, a lamp to my feet, and a light unto my path.

In my moments of inadequacy and tiredness, you ensured that the torch remained aflame to complete the work.

You have forever changed my life, and words cannot express the fullness of my heart.

Eternally grateful!

About the Author

Alean Smith is a multi-talented individual that uses her gifts and talents to inspire and cultivate others. She has an unwavering passion for guiding and mentoring the ingenious spirit of Millennials, Gen Z, and Gen Alpha concerning their purpose. She loves inspiring, teaching, and advising children and young adults to reach their full potential.

Introduction

Let's delve into a brief journey through a biblical narrative detailing a heinous plot and how God seated a divinely chosen heroine on the Persian throne to fulfill His plan. As we shift our focus to an era dominated by kings and kingdoms, we will spotlight the difference between man's wisdom and God's sovereignty and infinite wisdom. We will also observe the triumph of love, obedience, sacrifice, and selflessness over hatred and anger. Ultimately, we will witness a display of destiny pushing one into their most significant moment of triumph, leading them to their profound revelation of purpose.

We begin our journey with Esther, who became the Queen of Persia. She was married to Ahasuerus (also known as Xerxes the Great)—a Persian king who reigned from 486 B.C. to 465 B.C. The Persian empire was vast (stretching from India to Ethiopia). Ahasuerus hailed from a lineage of kings who ruled and influenced Near Eastern and European civilizations for over two centuries. The Persian elite ruled an empire that contained a melting pot of nations. Each practiced its religion and culture.

As one of the wealthiest and most influential kings in history, Ahasuerus displayed no restraint in flaunting his wealth. He ruled with supreme authority over his kingdom. Today, ladies, some would label Ahasuerus as a "baller." As the queen of this great king, Esther also possessed power, wealth, and influence. Yet, her most memorable moment as queen occurred when she displayed unwavering courage in the face of opposition. In an autocratic society, challenging the king or Persian Law resulted in severe punishment (sometimes banishment or even death). There was no exclusion for anyone, not even the queen.

Highlights and Facts about Esther

Brief Background	Esther's descendants were foreigners to Persia. They were exiled from their native land of Israel by a Babylonian king (Nebuchadnezzar), whose empire was later overthrown by the Persians.
Queen of Persia: Second wife to Ahasuerus	Vashti, Ahasuerus's first wife, was banished for refusing to appear before him at the king's banquet in a moment of rage. Esther was chosen as the new Queen of Persia.
Preparation for Queenship	Esther and the other young virgins each underwent a twelve-month preparation period.
Esther Favored	Esther won the favor of the king's servant, (Hegai), who oversaw the young women. He accelerated her beauty process and assigned seven

	female servants from the palace to serve her. Esther resided in the harem's best quarters.
Esther's Beauty and Character	**Esther's beauty complimented her bravery and character.**
Obedient and Teachable	**Esther was open to receiving counsel from her cousin Mordecai, who instructed her not to disclose her identity.**
Wise and Strategic	**Esther instructed her people to conduct a three-day fast before approaching the king to plead for herself and her people. She, along with her female servants, did the same.**
Courageous	**Driven by the purpose of saving her people, Esther violated Persian law by entering the inner court of the king's palace without permission.**
Divinely chosen as Queen	**God is Sovereign!**

The Brewing Of a Heinous Plot

What precisely initiated this heinous plot, and what was Esther's role? Esther learned of a decree to annihilate the Jewish race residing in Persia, orchestrated by Haman, the king's chief official. Haman's descendants were relentless in waging war against them, which ultimately led to their own demise. He especially despised Mordecai, Esther's cousin, who refused to bow and pay homage to him at the king's command. Mordecai would only give that kind of honor to God and was unwilling to compromise his stance. As a result, he became increasingly steadfast and determined to carry out his plan to rid Persia of those he considered a threat. Consumed with hatred, Haman made special provisions for the public execution of Mordecai. Inevitably, God thwarted Haman's plans, and his intent to hang Mordecai resulted in his fate. Esther and her people overcame their adversaries and celebrated with a great feast, and Mordecai attained a high position in the king's palace.

Before we applaud the heroic ending of this story, let us discuss the details of Esther's bravery, obedience, and selflessness. At Mordecai's request, Esther was instructed to go to the king and plead for the lives of all Jews living in Persia. "No big deal, right?" After all, she was the queen. However, the king had not summoned Esther, and it was forbidden to approach the king in the inner court without permission. The consequence was sudden death unless the king chose to extend his scepter. Esther was gripped with fear in that critical moment, initially causing her to respond unfavorably to Mordecai's request. However, driven by faith and a well-planned strategy, she mustered the strength and courage to risk it all. To undertake an impermissible action.

Esther fasted for three days, and on the third day, she dressed in royal clothing and entered the inner courtyard of the king's palace, where he was seated on his throne. She received favor to proceed forward, and he offered her up to half of his kingdom if that was her desire. Esther drew near to speak with the king but did not immediately reveal the urgency of the matter. Esther hosted two banquets for Haman and the king. During the second banquet, she unveiled Haman's wicked plan and earnestly pleaded for her life and the lives of her people.

"Phew!" I cannot fathom Esther's relief when the king granted her access to proceed forward, nor the joyous comfort of knowing that she and her family would live to face another day. How many of us could honestly say we would have followed through with Mordecai's request? Faced with such a decision, would you have packed your bags and run, or would you have taken Esther's stance, "If I perish, I perish?" God destined Esther to become queen; in that moment, I believe she discovered purpose in the journey. Perhaps Mordecai's reminder also resonated with her, prompting her to act upon her meaning for existing: "And who knows but that you have come to your royal position for such a time as this?" God used Esther to reveal his sovereignty and uphold a covenant with her forefathers. God will never allow man's laws to usurp His authority.

Esther may not have been the king's first choice as queen, but she was unquestionably God's choice. Envisioning an orphan, raised in exile, ascending to the throne of Persia would have been unthinkable. Esther's social status did not qualify her for influence. God operates according to His own will, and His plan always prevails. Esther was the answer to a pressing need, and her response to that need led to a victorious outcome. When the situation unfolded, resulting in man's decision to depose Vashti for refusing to appear at the king's banquet, God seized the opportunity to seat Esther into a position of power and authority to fulfill His divine plan. Although her royal heritage was initially concealed, God never discounted the fact, and He exalted her to a position of authority, even in a foreign land. It is impossible to decipher God's strategic plan unless He chooses to reveal His intentions.

Esther embraced her purpose by endangering her life to save an entire nation. When you surrender everything, your love, efforts, and actions, to God in accordance with His purpose, you cannot lose. God is omnipotent! Defeat will conquer failure when you are operating in His divine will.

Remember, your future is secure in Christ, and the outcome assuredly is a "win, win."

Part One

For All the Women

Chapter 1: Opposition vs. Opportunity

Resilience over Opposition!

In this field called life, I sometimes view myself as a quarterback holding the football. It is the fourth quarter, the final stretch, and the clock is winding down with a minute left in the game. My team and I are trailing by three points, waging on the verge of losing the championship game. The opposing team is already prematurely assuming victory. Yet, this is the game-winning drive for our chance to hoist the trophy, an opportunity to display our resilience.

As I take the snap, I drop back to survey the field. Indeed enough, opposition arises quickly! Out of nowhere, the opposing player delivers a vicious blow, and I crash to the ground. Caught off guard from the blind-sided tackle, I could only lie there as the opposition momentarily impeded my ability to move. I arise, return to my feet, and continue to move forward through the last few critical moments of the game.

Time and the opposing team tightened their grip on our chance for the win. Now, my mental resilience takes center stage!

Recognizing the dwindling time, I shift my focus to the next play. We must get in the end zone to score the much-needed touchdown. As the quarterback, the fear of another sack or even an interception arises. It is intimidating as I look at the number of opponents on the field trying to stop my team and me from making the touchdown. On the contrary, I can also see my offensive linemen. They cover me, giving me a clear view of finding my wide receiver who can carry the ball to gain yardage and eventually score. Unable to find an open teammate, I gain the tenacity to run the ball myself. There is an understanding that the ball must move forward. No matter what! A sudden burst of adrenaline and the hunger for the win forces my team and me to persevere until the last second to achieve victory. A sweet victory!

"Don't call it a comeback!" The tenacious fortitude to win has always existed and exists in you too! What is the game-winning life drive that motivates you to strive for success? Life's oppositions can force us to push through, stand, or fold. Our response in those final moments can drastically change the outcome. Trust me, sometimes, giving up or responding negatively to the opposition is easier. However, we must not allow those moments to steal our victories.

I know this can be challenging to practice, especially when our emotions arise. Our humanistic response to opposition is to "clap back" negatively instead of shaking it off and moving forward. Yes, it is necessary to refortify our defenses to prevent life's next tackle, but we must understand that timing and release are imperative. It is similar to a quarterback awaiting the perfect moment to release the ball into the hands of an open teammate or take off to scramble.

Let us delve into the meanings of "opportunity and opposition." Opportunity is defined in the dictionary as "a good chance for advancement or progress." Seizing opportunities helps build courage, perseverance, and strength, contributing to personal growth. Let us define "opposition," which is "the state of disagreeing with or disapproving of or the act of resisting." Opposition may manifest as fear, rejection, social pressures, and any other challenge that seeks to affect your growth. The good news is that God has equipped us with the necessary tools to confront and overcome the difficulties that stand against us.

Throughout my postgraduate tenure at Florida A&M University, I was regularly tasked with delivering oral presentations. I was confident of the presentation material, but the looming pressure to perform would often overshadow my confidence. Fear would settle in when a previous classmate delivered an excellent presentation, and I did not want to present behind them. The final grade was always favorable, but momentary fear instilled a false sense of inadequacy. The repeated cycle of presenting served as a valuable tool in overcoming anxiety related to public speaking. Opposition can also be constructive, as it reveals specific areas where training and cultivation are needed to boost self-confidence.

Life lessons usually occur after we have missed a good opportunity or made an unfavorable decision. It is wise to have a plan or strategy of execution when confronted with a task. I have learned to use wisdom by asking for guidance before undertaking an assignment or making a life-altering decision. I am continually reminded that God speaks to us in various ways concerning direction- through prayer, reading His word, or through mentors and teachers. The key is to maintain an open ear to hear the message of what He is attempting to convey.

When I think about Esther's opposition, my life's challenges seem trivial. As time passed, while in a sobering moment, the king reflected on the consequences of his decision to banish Queen Vashti. At the king's attendants' suggestion, a quest for a new queen occurred. Esther, along with numerous other young, beautiful virgins, were ordered by the most powerful man in the kingdom to leave their families to contend for one open position. There was no option to decline the request, and the women not selected as queen found themselves residing in the king's harem alongside the other concubines.

Picture your highlighted moment being viewed as "not good enough." Eventually, you and the other young women become an afterthought as time passes. Your destiny had been preordained the moment you were brought to the king's palace. Esther could have easily fallen victim to this predetermined fate, but God's plan for her was to become queen.

Secondly, had Esther not faced the daunting task of approaching the king, the recorded history of her life may not have been so triumphant. She, too, wrestled heavily with destiny and purpose but successfully turned opposition into opportunity. Life will present instances where we must choose to display courage and perseverance or remain unassertive and lose the opportunity for growth.

Mordecai also reminded Esther that if she were unwilling to plead for the lives of her people, deliverance would emerge from another place. Indeed, she and her family's house would be destroyed. Destroyed? How so, given Esther's status as queen? Esther did not reveal her ethnicity or birthplace to anyone at Mordecai's request. Consequently, when the deadly decree was issued, neither the king nor Haman knew the queen's true identity. Thus, her royal position alone would not have saved her. At times, overcoming opposition demands that we take risks beyond what is visible or imaginable, yet it becomes necessary to unlock our full potential for greatness.

The story of Esther is full of opposition and opportunity. Confronting the threat of annihilation can be deeply unsettling; nonetheless, with divine assistance, Mordecai and Esther rose to the occasion to defeat the opposing force that carefully plotted their downfall. Therefore, do not be discouraged or distracted by the opposition. You will experience resistance in this life, and your response will determine the outcome.

Taking risks requires a level of boldness and resilience. If God instructs us to approach Him boldly, especially in prayer, with our needs, we should not be meek and timid when confronted with life's challenges. Running the race set before us by God with all diligence allows our light to shine from within. God's spirit illuminates within us as a radiant beacon, drawing others towards us. Similar to a luxury car rotating on a showroom floor. I now view those moments in my life as character-building opportunities—an opportunity to transition and move forward into moments of destiny.

Opportunities can propel you into destiny, provided your mind, desire, and heart are open to God's will. So often, we find ourselves faced with tasks that seem unfitting and lack formal training in that area, and training is essential to maximize the opportunity entirely. I have encountered instances throughout my journey where God has trained and equipped me through the leading of the Holy Spirit. It required complete openness, receptiveness, and obedience to the voice of God, which is not always easy.

There is nothing comparable to God training and equipping you himself. The growth journey is challenging, but once you reach a level of maturity, the new version of yourself is undeniably remarkable. "Not that any man should boast in himself," but God extends unto us his grace and blesses our hands' work. Sometimes, there is no definitive training, and we must learn as we go. Let us take being a mom as an example. There is no "how to" guide for every parenting challenge. Sometimes, you must adapt to whatever comes along and deal with the obstacles as they arise. While preparation is necessary, there are moments when you cannot predict every detail.

In the face of opposition, your morality and courage will be tested, providing the stage to display your inner values. It will show your resilience as you maneuver through life's obstacle course. Moments will also occur to persuade you that you do not meet the specified qualifications nor have a right to belong in a setting that is pre-destined for you. Esther entered the scene long after Vashti was removed. Still, if we fast forward to today's society, where vanity takes center stage, we can quickly become clutched with fear and intimidation when we see what has been before us.

As a woman, it is easy to become ostracized if you do not meet societal standards of appearance. Our hair must be flawless, and we must possess a certain level of education to validate our skills. Although Esther received favor through preparation to become the next queen, I can only imagine the mixed emotions and thoughts running through her mind as a woman. To become the next Queen of Persia, having heard the fate of the one who went before you, would rightfully raise concerns. Despite being the most beautiful and influential woman in the kingdom, Vashti could not maintain her status as queen.

Let us be clear here! Women need to take pride in their appearance and exemplify good decorum. Real men are not interested in pursuing women who appear disheveled, unlearned, or defiant. However, do not let the outer appearance overshadow what truly matters. Vanity goes beyond physical appearance to include material possessions, such as cars, money, jobs, social status, etcetera. It is non-beneficial to trade destiny for vanity. True growth begins from within and radiates to our outer being. God created us to serve a specific purpose. He also designed us with inner sustenance to help us fulfill that purpose. Let us awaken the spirit of Esther within us, aspiring to become the complete package-mature and lacking nothing.

Growth opportunities are all around us. It is our responsibility to recognize and seize them. Choose to pursue those endeavors that align with the purpose in your heart. Some may wonder, "How will I know which opportunities are right for me?" Whenever an opportunity presents itself, I evaluate the effects of the potential outcome on me or someone else. If the opportunity has no value, then I do not pursue it. Some opportunities will present themselves, which are great, but make sure they are the right opportunities. Ask yourself: Does the opportunity align with my life's purpose? If it does not provide a sense of purpose, you are engaging in tasks that keep you in cycles of helping others without investing in yourself. The opportunity can also be a distraction that pulls you away from what you are supposed to pursue. I do not want to seem selfish, but it is about maintaining balance. Giving back and serving others is essential. My current goal is to pour into and assist you in your journey.

I have learned that we should not categorize all life occurrences of opposition as "negative." In fact, it can indicate that you are on the right path. I have shared some examples of my challenges throughout this chapter to support this statement. Let opposition strengthen your resilience. If the opposition challenges you to grow, continue moving forward on the current path. There is an adage from the older generation that I have heard consistently throughout my life. "If it was easy to get, it is probably not worth having."

Opposition also brings reflection! Reflecting on the hurdles we have overcome encourages and reinforces our faith for the next assignment. It is a signal that God is actively working on our behalf. If God orchestrated Esther's steps behind the scenes, we could trust Him to do the same for us. At times, I find myself amazed at what I can accomplish.

Overcoming opposition may cause momentary fatigue. I am learning the importance of allowing my mind and body to rest. Take time to relax and return to the task once you are refreshed. Your destiny is an ongoing journey, never complete for as long as you are living. Seize every opportunity and view opposition as a means to complete the "good work God began in you."

➢ List some oppositions that have prevented you from pursuing destiny. Now, list at least one opportunity or positive resolution for each to help you overcome that opposition. Once this is complete, congratulate yourself with a small celebratory moment. This is the first step forward towards the completion of your goals. Another step towards pursuing destiny.

➢ Reflect on some obstacles and challenges you have overcome (minor and significant). How did those victories encourage you to pursue your next goal or defeat your next challenge?

Scriptural Support Readings:

- Philippians 1:6 "I am sure of this, that He who started a good work in you will carry it on to completion until the day of Christ Jesus." [HCSB]

- Psalms 27:1 "The Lord is my light and my salvation-whom shall, I fear? The Lord is the stronghold of my life- of whom should I be afraid?" [HCSB]

- Isaiah 41:13 "For I, Yahweh your God, hold your right hand and say to you: Do not fear, I will help you." [HCSB]

- I John 5:14,15 "Now this is the confidence that we have before Him: Whenever we ask anything according to His will, He hears us. And if we know that He hears whatever we ask, we know that we have what we have asked Him for." [HCSB]

- Exodus 14:14 "The Lord will fight for you; you must be quiet." [HCSB]

- 2 Timothy 1:7 "For God has not given us a spirit of fearfulness, but one of power, love, and sound judgment." [HCSB]

- Philippians 4:13 "I am able to do all things through Him who strengthens me" [HCSB]

21

Chapter 2: Focus

"Let your eyes look forward: fix your gaze straight ahead."

- *Proverbs 4:25*

During my college days, I would try to find my friends at each football game. Knowing that my friends were in the same place to experience the camaraderie made game day attendance special. Fellowship with my friends is always a bonus that I cherish dearly, and it felt good to take a moment to enjoy this simple pleasure. Pinpointing their position was almost impossible with thousands of people in and around the stadium, so I would bring my binoculars to the game to find them. Even with the help of binoculars, I still needed to get them into focus to pinpoint their exact position. I would tune out the surrounding distractions and focus on the task at hand. Without fail, I managed to find each person seated in various locations throughout the stadium.

While writing to share this experience, I stopped to ask myself a question. What else could I accomplish if I applied this type of effort to focus on essential aspects of my life that needed my undivided attention? Specifics such as finishing this book, adopting a healthier lifestyle, or taking the time to focus on my well-being. Directing my attention to these areas would alleviate the stress of missing important deadlines and enhance my overall quality of life. I pose these types of questions to myself to stay motivated and focused.

Distractions can significantly influence our self-will to remain focused. These examples can hinder our ability to stay focused, whether they arise from relationships, unforeseen circumstances, social platforms, or temptations. Distractions are inevitable, but we cannot allow negative influences or thoughts to alter our decisions or affect our goals. Managing our thoughts and being intentional in our daily efforts are ways to help me overcome distractions.

It is said that the average attention span is around eight seconds, with the human brain able to focus up to ninety minutes before needing a break. This information is correct concerning my ability to focus. If you want my attention, the first ten seconds of your presentation or conversation are pivotal. Beyond that time limit, it becomes challenging for me to engage fully with what you are teaching or saying. The tasks I must complete that day will take precedence, and my mind wanders elsewhere as you are speaking to me.

Focusing also helps us to guard our eyes and ear gates. The digital world of information is immense, rapidly changing, and readily accessible. It connects people in many places, cultures, and arenas and can be an excellent resource for gathering prompt information. The information we collect, whether visual or audible, will shape our growth. Knowledge expansion is beneficial for achieving our goals, but we must be mindful of the type of information we consume and the time we spend on it. There must be a balance. As I age, I understand the importance of time management. Whether in a professional or spiritual context, we must manage our time wisely concerning the information we have access to.

Focus on a particular goal and strive to accomplish it. Focusing on a specific task helps stabilize your thoughts, actions, and emotions. This is important because we cannot hear from God or exercise rational thinking in the midst of chaos. It is enticing to roam free without a thought or care, but unchecked thoughts and desires can compromise our character. Let us reel in our thoughts and emotions to remain stable.

Our goals and accomplishments should align to please God, not what we can gain from them to bring self-notoriety. Replace self-notoriety with the posture of humility and servitude. Christ modeled this behavior to humanity. He never competed with his opponents. He possessed the power and authority of His Father in Heaven yet displayed humility, constraint, love, and obedience. Crowned as the "King of Kings," His name reigns supreme above every other name. Everyone (in heaven, on earth, and under the earth) "will know his name, bow their knee, and confess with their tongue that He is Lord." Now, that is a great victory, my friend!

Our character and integrity should be shaped by one ultimate source- God! Let Him be the motive for our success, and He will ensure abundance when we prioritize Him. Allow his desires to align with our own, as obedience, sacrifice, and submission to God have many rewards. Let us redirect our hearts and center our focus on God's will to experience true joy instead of temporary fulfillment.

Become A Visionary! (Focusing births Vision)

God has already written our destinies from start to finish. Our job is to discover what we were born to do, which requires vision. We must have the ability to see ourselves doing something constructive. Starting a business, graduating at the top of your class, home ownership, and pregnancy are all examples that require vision. I will use my niece as an example. She is currently seeking a degree in biochemistry and wants to own a bakery. She is exceptionally talented at baking and cooking. She is also motivated to graduate at the top of her class. During our conversation, she told me how she plans to execute each accomplishment. Determination and focus are motivating factors to ensure her vision becomes a reality.

Pregnancy and childbirth are other examples. It is standard practice for the expecting mother to have two fetal ultrasound exams to ensure a healthy baby during pregnancy. The exam shows images of your baby and helps the physician evaluate for growth and development. Your physician can also confirm the due date, determine the sex, examine your baby's heartbeat, look for a single baby versus multiple babies, and provide further screenings if needed. Envisioning your child's birth produces excitement and the need to prepare for this special gift from God. Along comes the gender reveal, the baby shower, and the vision of decorating the baby's room. The creation of life becomes actuality as you hold your bundle of joy. Your plans and living arrangements change as you focus on the needs of what you are now responsible for cultivating.

When our vision aligns with God's plans, we operate within the center of His will. Imagine standing on the peak of a mountain, and as you turn, you can see all angles, a panoramic view. You can see the clear roads and pitfalls, the places to stop and safely rest, and the places to speed through without hesitation. While specific details of the journey, whether in business, graduation, or motherhood, might seem distant, focusing allows us to catch a glimpse of the promise. Bringing our vision into focus gives us a clear sense of direction.

Dreaming Stimulates Vision!

My most memorable accomplishments began with a dream. In my quiet moments, I would focus on the aspirations in my heart. Subsequently, what I envisioned translated into written words on paper. Some seemed impossible, and just thinking about the project's challenges would encourage me to scratch the idea. The assignment's demands and daily life's responsibilities seemed overwhelming. Thankfully, taking another look at what was written would reignite my desire to push forward. As stated in an earlier chapter, I would ask God for a strategy for working out the vision. Nothing concerning God and his creation is trivial; he wants us to think big. We would never have access to some of the wonderful everyday inventions created for our use if someone had not pursued their "big idea." Work and produce the vision of what you see!

Lastly, let us discuss the Creator. Imagine creating an entire universe. The solar system, the elements, plants, creatures great and small, and above all, human life! It is almost impossible to comprehend the level of detail involved in creating something so meticulous. The undertaking was tremendous yet well executed. God's artistry of creation is the epitome of perfection, so much so that he blessed and sanctified his work. God gave us the blueprint in the book of Genesis of the meaning of "work ethic." He also completed his work from creation with rest.

No one else in history has modeled that kind of capability and instruction. The word "accomplishment" would unjustly describe that level of detailed work. God created man in His image, so consider the possibilities of what we can achieve. Bringing our vision into focus enables us to create the unimaginable, evolving into beautiful artistry shaped by the Creator.

- ➢ List some goals/assignments you are working on and others that have been put on hold and need completion.

- ➢ List some distractions that are preventing you from focusing on your goals/assignments.

- ➢ Write a resolution or plan of how to proceed with completing that goal/assignment.

- ➢ Prioritize each goal/assignment.

- ➢ Create a vision board with the listed goals. Check off each goal once you complete them.

- Matthew 6:33: "But seek first the kingdom of God and His righteousness, and all these things will be provided for you." [HCSB]

- I Corinthians 10:13: "No temptation has overtaken you except what is common to humanity. God is faithful, and He will not allow you to be tempted beyond what you are able, but the temptation He will also provide a way of escape so that you are able to bear it." [HCSB]

- 2 Corinthians 4:18: "So we do not focus on what is seen, but on what is unseen. For what is seen is temporary, but what is unseen is eternal." [HCSB]

- Habakkuk 2:2,3: "Write down this vision; clearly inscribe it on tablets so one may easily read it. For the vision is yet for the appointed time; it testifies about the end and will not lie. Though it delays, wait for it since it will certainly come and not be late." [HCSB]

- Matthew 7:7: "Keep asking, and it will be given to you. Keep searching, and you will find it. Keep knocking, and the door will be opened to you." [HCSB]

Chapter 3: Transforming Your Mindset

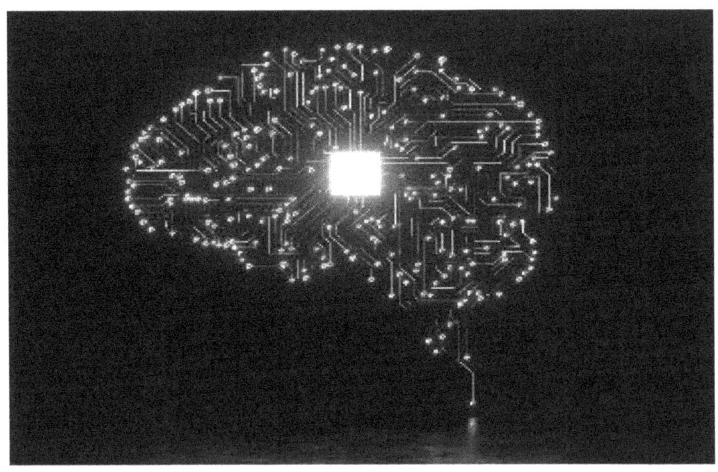

"Do not be conformed to this age, but be transformed by the renewing of your mind, so that you may discern what is the good, pleasing, and perfect will of God."

- Romans 12:2

Of all of God's creations, he created man who could exercise freedom of thought. Our cultivated thoughts will lead to actions that influence who we become and how we view life. We should protect our hearts, eyes, eargates, and thoughts. Our thoughts and words we speak hold the power to influence the outcome in terms of progress and creativity.

Had God spoken of authoring this book ten years ago, I surely would have laughed and run for cover. Being utterly transparent about my flaws to others would have been a "No 10-4 Good Buddy!" Revelation concerning my destiny manifested at the right time, as submission to His will had become my heart's desire. I began the challenge of something new, and the teacher became the student again. I needed to prepare for the intense preparation and guidance that filled my life. I had to adjust to meet the demands of my purpose. Be ready when you tell God you are prepared for the next step!

Submission, trust, and faith all play a role in renewing the mind. Let us define submission. Submission is: "the act of yielding your authority or will to another." The trust factor is also essential, as submission requires us to be vulnerable. Submission conveys the following: "I am completely yielding my authority to you, trusting that you will not abuse it." That is huge! Trust is what keeps us connected to God. We can always trust him. When our relationships crumble, man will expose our flaws, but God will not mishandle what we choose to surrender to him. His thoughts toward us are always good, and he intends to provide us with "hope and a future."

Women are instinctively nosy about particular situations. We want to see, know, and understand what we are signing up for before committing. Indeed, that is a wise decision, but what happens on those rare occasions when the opportunity is unavailable for vetting? God desires you to have it, but are you willing to release control, or would you pass up the opportunity? Again, trust at this level requires faith.

Now, let us define faith. Faith is: "the reality of what is hoped for, the proof of what is not seen." As a believer in God's word, I view faith as "a trust or assurance of God's promises in His word for the things that are not visual to the eye." My friends and I refer to it as a "free fall." Faith can and will defy reasoning, especially when you believe for something tangible to occur that you cannot see.

I can attest again to this statement while writing this book. Emotions of fear and doubt began to infiltrate my mind. Thoughts of "what if the material is not good enough, or what if some reject it because you are not a seasoned author." With other projects, opposition would often arise, attempting to sow doubt. Esther, too, had to change her way of thinking. Assuming the responsibility of ruling a kingdom and developing a successful strategy to approach the king required such a change. Either we trust God completely or forfeit the greatness he put inside us. We must decide! Once you have taken the leap of faith and discovered that the benefits far exceed the risks, it boosts your confidence for the next task.

Some of you may find this mindset to be challenging. Your rebuttal response may sound familiar to this statement, "well, I tried to start the business, but it failed, or I have tried school, and it just did not work for me at that time." The good news is that you can always try again. The road to success is not always easy, but opposition eventually moves when we operate in our God-given gifts and talents. Reflecting on my journey, I have learned that many of life's obstacles resulted from my actions. I did not understand the power of positive thinking and how it would have accelerated my progress during the early stages of young adulthood. Today, I realize that even one moment of hesitation can breed fear and negative thinking, and that kind of mindset hinders growth.

There will be times when life will not align with our plans. God's word reminds us "not to be conformed to this world, but to be transformed by the renewing of our minds." When negative thoughts occur, I remind myself of God's words concerning my challenging situations. Following that, I prioritize and pursue the opportunities that bring positive changes. I pray, reflect quietly, and assess where I want to be.

Regarding my future, I considered it unwise to embark upon my thirties without a clear idea of who I wanted to become. I believed that If I did not have a plan by that age, others would attempt to dictate what I should be doing and who I should become. I needed to take control of my life early on because I was a people pleaser and would have sacrificed my dreams and ambitions. Making smart decisions helped me to identify my strengths and weaknesses, shaping and molding my character. I must confess, the dumb decisions helped as well. They helped me understand who I did not want to become. It is surprising that even now, some of those reflections can bring a terrible shock to my brain as I attempt to suppress those inerasable moments. I quietly reply to myself from within, "Girl, what were you thinking back then."

That was not a story for the grandkids or anyone else. Those moments are most private (as you chuckle to yourself). Your lips become sealed as you bury the thought deep within your mind.

Resolving my issues using the suggestions of the world's system resulted in significant failures. Those suggestions were temporary solutions to solving my internal battles. It was challenging to face my mind battles because it forced me to self-invent my insecurities. Insecurities that lingered and eventually became a mental stronghold that was almost impossible to defeat. It was challenging to defeat because I layered my stronghold with coverings of excuses and unfounded truths.

Can you imagine living life in a continuous state of emptiness? We have painted illusions of grandeur for everyone else to see, yet the unveiling exposes a depleted and tired individual ready to walk away from it all. Your frustration has reached its peak as ambition tries to drive you forward. Those frustrations have also connected with the mental stronghold. Tell me, what are you willing to relinquish in exchange for peace?

"Truly changing your mindset will reveal both the positive and negative aspects of your life." It tests your sincerity for change. I am thankful for my relationship with a loving and merciful God. Understanding the Creator's love towards his creation is almost incomprehensible. I seek God's vision for the desired outcome when mental opposition arises. As stated earlier, if I can see the result through His perspective, I can steamroll through the internal opposition and stay on the course of my destiny.

Picture overcoming the internal struggles within our mind. In that case, we can shatter the thick glass ceiling to obtain the beautiful opportunities waiting at the next level. While the shattered glass may cause bruising and cuts, we gain access to operating in a dimension of endless possibilities once the healing occurs. God predestines our lives for a specific purpose, but we must be willing to act upon what we discover. What do you desire concerning your future? Are you willing to change your mindset to pursue your vision? Believe in yourself because you are internally stronger than you think.

Transforming Your Mindset

Meditation Moment Exercise

Today, take a few moments to sit quietly and clear your mind. Meditate on a goal or opportunity that would change the course of where you are in life. Think of the benefits and open doors the opportunity could bring. Imagine yourself in that space, engaging in the very thing you desire. The power of positive thinking will help you to pursue what you have envisioned.

➤ Philippians 3:13,14: "Brothers, I do not consider myself to have taken hold of it. But one thing I do: Forgetting what is behind and reaching forward to what is ahead, I pursue as my goal the prize promised by God's heavenly call in Christ Jesus" [HCSB]

➤ Proverbs 3:5,6: "Trust in the Lord with all your heart, and do not rely on your own understanding; think about Him in all your ways, and He will guide you on the right paths" [HCSB]

➤ Proverbs 16:3: "Commit your activities to the Lord, and your plans will be achieved" [HCSB]

➤ Ephesians 4:23: "You are being renewed in the spirit of your minds, you put on the new self the one created according to God's likeness in righteousness and purity of the truth" [HCSB]

➤ Matthew 10:39: "Anyone finding his life will lose it, and anyone losing his life because of Me will find it." [HCSB]

Chapter 4: The Road Less Traveled

"Think about Him in all your ways, and He will guide you on the right paths."

- Proverbs 3:6

While pursuing destiny, there will come a point where you will encounter a fork in the road: comfort versus purpose. One can choose the familiar path of comfort or take an adventurous detour toward a new course that awaits. Embracing destiny brings unexpected life changes that are essential for growth. One we must embrace if we desire to evolve. After submitting to destiny's call, I encountered a roadblock along my current path, redirecting me into unchartered territory. Closed doors of the past became a reality, paving the way for God's favor to materialize through newfound opportunities in various forms.

This new route seemed beautiful and exciting in the early stages of preparation. A fresh new scenic route on a canopy road with a variation of shaded trees and a calming view of a weeping willow by the lake gleaming from the sunlight in the near distance. My new plan for achieving my goals worked well, and I saw results quickly. I accelerated out of my scenic route into broad open terrain. I was now pursuing destiny at full throttle, and completing specific projects manifested quickly due to the decrease in my hours of sleep.

The desire to see my goals become a reality superseded the need for sleep. I had written several goals for myself during that season. I began to work a few at a time to prevent feeling overwhelmed, but the more I completed, the harder I pushed myself. During that time, I returned to school to obtain additional certifications, wrote a children's play, and created several short animation videos. I also began to pen songs I would hear while sleeping. It was an inspiring time as those gifts burst forth simultaneously.

Surely enough, I began checking off completed projects from my vision board. A sense of accomplishment, purposeful living, and humility emerged. I am feeling "pretty good" about myself at the moment. Life is good! Unfortunately, those moments are often temporary, as opposition finds a way to surface at the most unwanted times. Once again, the scenery changes in the middle of my training and preparation. A route change along the destination required me to navigate into unfamiliar terrain, forcing me to choose an alternate route.

Upon entrance, I proceeded down a canyon road with rocky terrain, and the stable surroundings I was accustomed to seemed to vanish. The rocks atop the canyon seemed unstable and looked like they might tumble down any second. Additionally, a sudden rainstorm forced me to decelerate tremendously. Everything that I had diligently pursued up to this point was threatening abortion. While passionately pursuing destiny, I unexpectedly fell ill. Other stable aspects of my life were in pandemonium as well. Work was crazy, an attack on my family arose, and I was trying to manage multiple situations simultaneously.

What do you do when the road less traveled forces you to trust God's plan without an apparent escape or exit route? Despite consulting physicians, undergoing multiple tests, and even having surgery, there were no conclusive answers. I could not understand why I was experiencing sickness at this time in my life. I had always been in good health with no serious issues. Indeed, if the experts had no clue what was happening internally, I was clearly at a loss for how to proceed. I only knew that I was in a fight for my life. My sickness caused both physical and emotional fatigue. Without a change, the white banner of a forfeit in the form of a U-turn would become inevitable. Now that I ponder the thought, forfeiting at that point was not an option either. I had advanced too far to turn around; it would have been unbelievable to do so. In His wisdom, God knows when to allow us to be tested.

I began loosening the grip on the steering wheel. I was going down due to the exhaustion of the fight. I could not keep any food in my stomach. It was as if food were a foreign body, and my digestive system would reject it. So, I lost my desire to eat because I did not want to get sick. I began losing weight rapidly like Mike Tyson dropping his opponents with a TKO in the boxing ring. I shed over sixty pounds during this season of sickness.

Unfortunately, not eating caused a domino effect of other minor health issues. These issues included severe acne outbreaks due to decreased fluid intake and iron deficiency anemia, leading to severe fatigue. I began receiving intravenous iron treatments twice a week. The human body has a complex immune system. Its purpose is to fight foreign invasions, but during this time, it seemed as if it was non-responsive to its warring opponents.

What do you do when facing a storm that you can share with no one else? My life has always been private. I only share my life experiences with close friends and family, and I chose to withhold the need to share this information from most of them, including my mom. I should have known not to conceal this illness from Mom. Those maternal bloodhound instincts would soon discover my internal battle. I would try to reassure her that I was fine, but she would look me in the face and reply, "A mother always knows when there's something wrong with her child."

The factors mentioned above were significant, but my breaking point came when the sickness took its toll on my mental health, which caused me to spiral downward. It felt as if I was on a never-ending roller coaster, and thoughts of when and if this storm would pass began to affect my faith and belief in healing. You see, it is easy to confess that you believe in God for healing or a miracle when you are not in a moment of testing, but what is your response when you truly need God's deliverance? Is your faith easily wavered by the quandary of doubt within your mind, or is it anchored solidly due to your belief in God's word for healing? Every man is given a measure of faith, but can you believe God for the gift of faith for healing when the days turn into weeks? The lingering weeks turn to months, and nearly two years have passed without signs of deliverance.

Many days, I would lie across my bed in tears due to the pain, and as I slipped into sleep mode, I would pray for healing. I did not want to experience another day like the previous one. I wanted my quality of life back. Who wants to exist and not experience life to its fullest? I had to signal an SOS beacon to Heaven, as there were moments when I wanted to stop praying and give up. I find solace in knowing that my creator wanted me to live when I lost faith and reassurance. Broken moments! How do you face and win a fight with yourself to live? You versus You!

I began to renew my mind and confront this burdened season with persistent prayer. Instead of asking someone to pray for me, I had to bombard Heaven for myself. I had to bear my own burden of sickness. There were moments when I wanted to reach out to someone, or anyone, who could get a prayer through to Heaven. It seemed my prayers were going unanswered concerning my sickness, which caused me to think differently. I never understood the meaning of intercession until this moment in life. I had read about it but needed more motivation to delve deeper for a proper understanding. Of course, prayer was a part of my daily life, but not to this extent. Family and building my career were my priorities. This experience revealed the need to reposition my priorities.

The affliction and attacks strengthened my prayer life. As I prayed God's words for healing, I gained further insight that this battle was not just about me. While receiving iron treatments for anemia at a cancer treatment center, I observed others undergoing various treatments, including chemotherapy. This prompted me to ask why I was in that setting when I did not have cancer. Revelation came that I was to pray for them, too. So, I started bringing my prayer book and praying silently for those alongside me. I would continue praying until I drifted off to sleep since my treatments lasted for two hours.

I was experiencing the best and worst times of my life. Cultivation of my inner being was transforming rapidly while an assailing downturn in my physical health unfolded. Your most remarkable moments of growth will happen within the darkest of times. Like a seed planted in the dirt, the sprouting process only appears once cultivated within the soil that covers it. I had to renew my mind daily and concentrate on what my new day would bring. God's mercies are new every morning, and his grace is sufficient for any challenges that arise. When my mindset changed, so did my situation. I consciously decided to surrender all to God, including the affliction and mind battles. It required selflessness and trust in God regardless of the outcome. Opposition can force you into a place where you must completely trust God. As time passes, you will see that it worked in your favor. While going through your trial, God will use it as a testimony to uplift someone else.

Surrendering to God will always be the wisest choice. I would have missed the enjoyable experience of knowing and nurturing my grandchildren, and the thought of my mother enduring the loss of yet another child would have been utterly unbearable. No amount of comfort could have eased her pain. Past losses caused me to grieve alongside her, witnessing a piece of her vanish each time she said goodbye. Opting to be the fifth of seven children to leave prematurely was not an option. How we live impacts our family and close connections, so choose wisely. Also, my forty-plus years of life would have served no valid purpose if I were unwilling to allow God to complete "the good works he began in me."

Shortly after, my health improved, and the 18-month illness ended. Before departing this rugged path, other aspects of my life had stabilized. It was satisfying to resume my journey when the sickness forced me to pause. I continued along a scenic route, passing open fields and trees adorned with fresh spring flowers. The clouds broke, and a rainbow appeared.

So, what did I discover on this road less traveled into destiny? At times, you may feel stuck once you realize the path you were on was essential to fulfilling your purpose. It is fuel for the writing machine that is inside of you. A person's life story could inspire someone else to persevere. They, too, faced significant challenges arising from unknown obstacles presented on their destiny path. With God's help, we can navigate life's unexpected challenges through prayer and perseverance. Situations and circumstances will catch us by surprise, but God already knew they would occur. He has already equipped us to be victorious. I can relate to the scripture in God's word that assures us, "All things work together for the good of them that love Him."

This journey has also helped me recognize that I could not continue navigating life thinking I was self-sufficient. God always provides a witness who can share the trials and victories that propel your growth. He appoints someone to tread the muddy trenches of life alongside you, praying for you when you cannot muster the strength to do so. They can empathize and share your pain when you cannot articulate what you are feeling or experiencing.

This route was joyous and fruitful, sometimes uncomfortable and painful, yet necessary to grow. Remaining on my familiar path would have resulted in laziness and complacency. There would have been no sense of urgency to cultivate the inner potential awaiting release. Pursuing destiny requires work, and challenging work is a requirement for success. Indeed, working smarter and not harder is essential, but without investing the necessary time and effort, you will always remain with the question of "what if."

On this journey, my sickness often confined me to home as I lacked the energy and strength to socialize with others. At other times, I immersed myself in accomplishing my goals and had no desire to break away and waste time partaking in something that had no benefit. Instead, I utilized that time to concentrate on the objectives outlined on my vision board. If I wanted clarity on how to proceed with specific projects, I needed to be alone to receive instruction on moving forward. This path has the potential to awaken dormant spiritual gifts. Have you ever experienced the incredible feeling of God speaking to you during quiet reflection? It is a powerful experience that can leave you with a sense of peace and clarity.

My pain served a purpose as well. It increased my compassion for others confronting challenges on the path to destiny. I have learned the importance of interceding with prayer on their behalf. Along this journey, I also learned that greatness costs. It may demand sleepless nights, unveil your devoted friends, reveal your internal strengths, test your sanity, and lead you into a season of isolation.

Even Esther paid a cost for receiving the crown. She had to leave her family and the comfort of her secure surroundings to prepare for a path she did not choose. As queen, she defied Persian law, which could have resulted in the loss of her life. Shakespeare's notable quote, "Uneasy lies the head that wears a crown," resonates suitably in Esther's situation. What cost are you willing to pay in your pursuit of purpose?

"Side note." Once you have weathered life's storms that have pushed you into your dimension of greatness, stand firm and do not let anyone diminish your achievements. Only you know the cost, and when faced with negative comments, kindly smile and leave them wondering. The glory of your success will serve as your receipt, and your life will testify to the sacrifices made. As God's word says, "A city sitting on a hill cannot be hidden." Never be ashamed to let the transformative work that God has accomplished within you shine through you. You represent Christ and belong to the only eternal kingdom.

Stepping into destiny often takes you in a completely different direction. God used an ordinary damsel for a remarkable and memorable task. Esther is just one historical example. The Bible offers other instances, such as Nehemiah, a cupbearer who led the rebuilding of Jerusalem, or David, a shepherd boy who became one of Israel's greatest kings. Obedience often requires undertaking unimaginable tasks, stretching your capabilities, comprehension, and, most importantly, faith.

I pray that my experiences, and those briefly mentioned above, inspire you to trust God, regardless of what lies ahead. Endure through your preparation process as "The Road Less Traveled" plays a vital role in your journey of self-discovery. The outcome can lead you to a beautiful destination. Once more, had I not been open to risking failure and exploring new possibilities, we would not have shared this experience. I would not have displayed divine nature- the inner strength that unleashes a mighty roar, compelling free will to align with destiny and make the right decisions.

Life's occurrences, preceding and following our discovery of purpose, contribute to our pursuit of it. It is all part of God's master plan. One might say that we each take the road less traveled. If you sense that life is calling you to something more purposeful, do not be afraid to embrace change and confront the challenge.

For those who have not chosen the path toward destiny, you have now reached a point where you must decide. Now that you have read this chapter, you have a level of accountability to try something different.

➢ Make a list of interests you have wanted to try or pursue.

➢ Act upon at least one of those interests and set a timeline to reach it.

➢ What will you leave behind to choose a different path for a fresh start?

Scriptural Support Readings

- Ecclesiastes 9:11: "Again I saw under the sun that the race is not given to the swift, or the battle to the strong, or bread to the wise, or riches to the discerning, or favor the skillful, rather, time and chance happen to all of them." [HCSB]

- Matthew 7:13: "Enter through the narrow gate. For the gate is wide and the road is broad that leads to destruction, and there are many who go through it." [HCSB]

- Psalms 90:17: "Let the favor of the Lord our God be on us: establish for us the work of our hands-establish the work of our hands." [HCSB]

- Proverbs 12:24: "The diligent hand will rule, but laziness will lead to forced labor" [HCSB]

- Jeremiah 29:11 "For I know the plans I have for you"-this is the Lord's declaration- "plans for your welfare, not for disaster, to give you a future and a hope." [HCSB]

- Isaiah 43:19: "Look, I am about to do something new, even now it is coming. Do you not see it? Indeed, I will make a way in the wilderness, rivers in a desert." [HCSB]

- Lamentations 3:22,23: "Because of the Lord's faithful love we do not perish, for His mercies never end. They are new every morning; great is Your faithfulness! [HCSB]

Chapter 5: Matters of the Heart

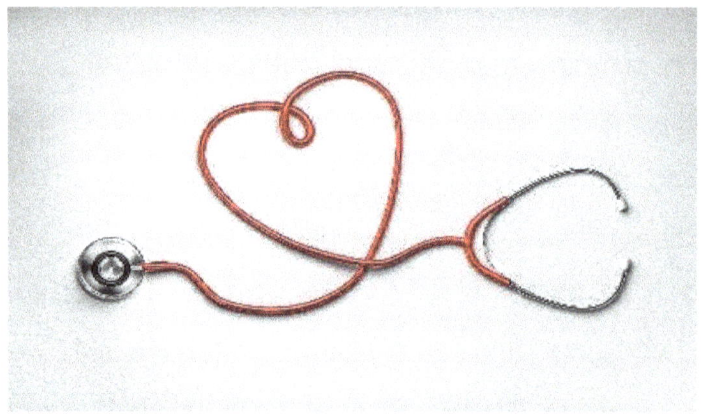

"Guard your heart above all else, for it is the source of life."

-   Proverbs 4:23

When I studied anatomy in college, I became fascinated with the heart. The heart is one of the body's most valuable organs. It is a powerful muscle that performs several functions to sustain life. The heart is centrally located in our physical being and is the primary organ of the Circulatory System. The heart replenishes depleted oxygen and rids the body of carbon dioxide and other wastes. It pumps oxygenated blood and nutrients out into different body systems so they may function properly. Not only does the heart perform the above tasks, but it also has a sound. Physicians use a stethoscope to assess whether the heart functions correctly or if any concerns may require further workup.

Just as the heart is significant to our physical body, it works simultaneously with the mind to control our emotions, intellect, and self-will. We have previously discussed the importance of our thoughts, but let us examine how they affect the heart. The heart responds to those thoughts relevant to our decision-making, so our mind matters become heart matters. Let us look at some instances to see how the above emotional and mental components resemble the physical heart's function.

Our kids, family, and friends hold the power to pull our heartstrings. Family plays a vital role in my daily life; I believe this is true for many others. Our reactions often mirror the heart's function when we are hurting or depleted. Let us consider our kids again to illustrate this statement further. My friend was devastated when her son broke his arm playing football. She ensured that he received the proper care and aided in nursing the arm back to health. Once his shoulder healed, she allowed him to return to the same game that caused them a season of discomfort.

When a mother hears her newborn crying through the baby monitor, it signals that her little one needs attention. As they age, she listens for laughter. This sound assures her that they are happy and well. As parents, we spare no expense concerning school tuition, graduation events, birthday parties, weddings, or any special occasion that emphasizes our children's special day. Our kids are a constant source of replenishment for the heart.

As we progress through this chapter, we will discuss various heart matters and their ultimate relation to love, so let us delve deeper into its importance. Love is an essential element in conversations about the heart. Love is conceived in the mind but takes on a physical form. As mentioned earlier, people's actions are shaped by their beliefs. Love is not only an emotion but a conscious choice that determines the value of the relationship, whether with friends, family, or a partner. When trouble arises in the relationship, deciding to continue loving the individual or part ways is crucial. Therefore, be intentional about the individuals you allow in your space, as commitments can be long-lasting or temporary.

The most remarkable book ever written, and its creator provides the most stunning example of love. God emphasizes its significance at length. There are at least three hundred occurrences of the word "love" throughout various bible translations. The concept of love, its characteristics, and its actions or inactions are illustrated in several sacred texts. God demonstrated his love for humanity by sending us His son to exemplify love and to redeem humanity from sin. What loving parent would sacrifice their child to save another? Even if the selfless deed ensured the survival of humanity. He proved to us that unconditional love always prevails despite the worldly opinions or actions of others!

Situations and circumstances will arise to test our inner being, and the heart will always testify to its true intent. I often remind my generation, Millennials and Gen Z, that "love" is an action verb. It not only speaks but also "does." People's thoughts and intentions are revealed by their actions and expressions. It is wise to listen when the heart speaks, whether good or harmful. The contents of a person's heart are often expressed verbally. One can make better decisions by paying attention to what is being said.

Observing a person's actions can also help you decide whether you desire a personal or professional relationship. Watch them closely because maintaining personal relationships takes effort. To do it properly, one must invest time, energy, devotion, and commitment. I do not seek friendship from those unwilling to pay the price. We, too, must be prepared to shoulder this responsibility.

Setting boundaries in love and relationships is a sensible choice, as we should not let our hearts cloud better judgment. This commonly occurs among women. My eighteen-month-old grandson, son, and daughter-in-law came home to visit after a year away in Hawaii. Their return filled my heart with joy. Soon enough, my grandson began to disrupt my peaceful space. I could not resist letting him explore freely. His little hands grabbed objects so swiftly that seeing what he had confiscated was difficult. Of course, my son would give me disapproving looks, but secretly, I enjoyed watching his journey of discovery. It was fascinating to see him quickly learn new things. He watched you complete a task and immediately modeled what he saw.

After a week of picking up paper clips, highlighters, and printer paper, I had to close the office playground. Today, at the tender age of eight and with two more grandchildren, I must limit the fun at Gigi's. Let us not pretend I am the only one who becomes a softie concerning our kids and grandkids. Call me impartial, but the love for our grandkids is even stronger than the love for our children.

I, too, am learning to restrain love. We end up raising Chuckie instead of Chuck when it spirals out of control. Entitlement begins to develop because we give them whatever they desire. Their once adorable smiles lose charm as their teenage years occur. It is no longer enduring when they feel the need to express their unwanted opinions. The loving mom's voice changes to firm and authoritative, and the change in your demeanor signals their need to be quiet and leave the room. Once they exit the room, you find yourself standing there, confused, questioning how you reached that point. This scenario is just one example. There are others that we can apply when interacting with our kids.

Now, let us re-direct our focus and discuss dead-end relationships. These relationships do not result in positive outcomes or bring positivity into your space. Dead-end relationships may lead you to lonely places, introduce you to counterfeits, bring rejection, and tempt you to settle due to the rejection. Counterfeits can come in various forms. A couple of examples include dead-end jobs and choosing the wrong mate.

I did not understand love, self-validation, or self-worth in my youth. My male counterparts would easily dominate, manipulate the relationship, and break the bond of trust. I was naive to equate sex with love, thinking that if I gave myself physically and emotionally, I would receive the same response. However, we now know this is not the case.

Bad relationships became a repetitive process. I could detect early in the relationship when it would not work. I knew the relationships were destined to fail, and I would be left to deal with the aftermath. I allowed the fear of being alone to overpower my intuition. Despite my partner's lack of desire for equal partnership, I adopted false hope that the next relationship would be different and would not fail. I formed soul ties with others who were not compatible, thus leaving me empty. Ladies, you cannot force a man to be loving, faithful, or truthful. His relationship with Christ keeps him loyal to his family and vows, shaping his character.

Imagine connecting a mismatched rib to a rib cage. Out of desperation, we glue or tape it in its proper place. It temporarily holds, but it causes significant discomfort. Eventually, it either breaks or wounds us badly, and we must release it. The repetitive process has now produced a deformed and dysfunctional rib cage. There is no recognition of how it is supposed to look, and it has lost its ability to protect the heart. Reconstruction is necessary to restore the rib cage to its original form. Now, we must find a way to release the soul ties of each counterfeit before we can receive one suitable for us.

The Pigpen Syndrome is what I have come to call such incidents in my life. I stayed in the Pigpen because I did not know my value as a woman. I was sinking further and deeper into the mire of failed relationships. I started to feel at ease just lying there, all filthy and malodorous. Not only did I not smell anything, but my vision was blurry. My self-perception was no more than what I allowed others to define me as. I had not taken the time to discover my strengths, gifts, and what I had to offer to myself and others." My self-worth was based on my outer appearance, and I used professional success to measure and validate my identity. I could never love someone else until I understood the true meaning of love and loving myself.

My mother and I never had "the talk" about love, males, and valuing oneself when I was young. Indeed, I could have avoided some of my confusion and suffering had I known better. Mom often reassured me that I was beautiful and brilliant, but I never believed her. I thought Mom told me those things to make me feel special as her daughter. I did not want to break the news to inform her that her model student was secretly engaging in some rather immoral acts. Why not?

Most of my friends were doing the same thing, and it looked like they were winning.

Albeit, I had a healthy fear of mom. My life would have hung in the gallows had I brought any shame or disgrace upon her house. So, I lived just on the edge of borderline riskiness. I did not fear God much then, but I indeed feared Margaret. It is now funny how those roles have flipped. My mom is old school, and other topics were not discussed in our home. As a Christian, sex before marriage should not have been an option anyway. This principle was clearly stated in our household.

When hormones and curiosity take over adolescent brains, what do you do? Today's youth still confront these issues and many more like them. Only now have they intensified to an extreme, making it difficult for us parents to understand. Social platforms make it convenient for them to find the answers elsewhere, whether positive or negative. To make things more complicated, they turn to their peers for answers.

As mothers and role models, we need to be open-minded about the struggles our teenagers experience. Today's world is much different from when we were young. We must find a way to connect with our teens. If we do not, they may confide in others for guidance as they navigate life. I am not trying to persuade you to abandon your principles. These requirements must not change under any circumstances. Our responsibility is to nurture them, but we must be personable and approachable. Their intelligence and desire to learn have surpassed our own at a similar age. They have challenged us to provide answers to some tough questions far sooner than anticipated.

This concept also applies to dead-end jobs. Despite spending many hours on weekly projects, more is needed to provide a sense of personal gratification. The current position you are working in does not display your skills. Sure, it pays the bills, but it is sucking the life from you, leaving you frustrated and emotionally spent. No energy is left to pursue your passion after taking care of personal and family responsibilities. Just thinking about it while in the moment eliminates the desire to add another task to a full plate.

Dedication becomes challenging when you discover that your current role serves no purpose with future destiny. I view this discovery as the Snow-White Effect. One has been spiritually sleeping ever so eloquently, and a destiny kiss from God awakens us from our dormant state to discover a new dimension of untapped potential. The career you loved and thought would produce greatness eventually becomes an undesirable, passionless routine, forcing you to re-evaluate your current state. I often hear this familiar storyline as I counsel women in this area. Women are competitive and aim for career success, but we must evaluate where we are if we desire to dominate in our God-given talents.

Purpose can be frustrating, but it serves as the driving force to pursue what intensely calls your name. Do you bravely close the door to comfort and security to risk it all? Eventually, you must! What you do can no longer take the driver's seat. Until you discover who you are, what you do will continue to be your driving force. The road of uncertainty can be a fearful route without God's guidance. You must ask God for wisdom on how and when to progress forward.

Let us shift once more to discuss rejection. Rejection hurts and can cause brokenness, and open rejection will make you run and wish that no one ever knew your name. It can cut so deep that the very thought will leave you speechless. We must not run but find the courage to stand and confront the issue.

In my younger years, I constantly desired to fit in, to be a validated part of something great. There was always something special and unique about Alean, but she could not see it due to her previous dealings with counterfeits. I would attempt to settle by compromising my standards despite what I knew that I deserved to have. Maturity and growth revealed that Alean was not designed to fit in. I now embrace being the misfit kid in the room because I know who I am. Even today, I still experience rejection and quickly remind myself of who I am. If my acceptance is unwanted, it is the other person's loss. I do not stop to justify my worth to anyone. Time is a valuable commodity and, every moment in life matters.

Truth moment! There are times when we play a role in the rejection we experience. Let me elaborate on a couple of statements from the previous paragraph concerning my desire to compromise my standards. Intuition would let me know when the opportunity was unfavorable for a relationship and when I should not to engage. Still, I entertained the possibility and chose to ignore the warning signs. Whenever I override better judgment (or what my spirit is speaking), and the outcome is rejection, I must not blame the other person for the unfavorable outcome. Instead, I must take the loss and deal with what I could have prevented. This truth is a harsh reality yet a needed revelation for growth in building viable relationships. When rejection occurs due to our refusal to disengage, we must forgive ourselves and learn from the experience to heal.

Do not feel disheartened if you experience rejection. Reflecting on the situation can assist you with moving forward. Let us discuss an effective way to overcome rejection. We defeat the spirit of rejection by relying on God's word. God assures us that we are more than conquerors, fearfully and wonderfully made, and if He is for us, who can stand against us? Love is the appropriate response to rejection instead of bitterness and anger. Taking on Christ's characteristics helps us develop self-control instead of acting upon the arising emotion.

The statement, "hurt people hurt other people," has been quoted several times by well-known authors. I was reading a book about hurt and healing during my leisure time. If the person does not heal from the pain of rejection, that person can transform from victim to villain. The individual suppresses the pain instead of releasing it. The author defined a villain as "one who transfers their inner hurt onto others, and all the while, the individual continues to play the role of the victim." The villain uses their hurt to justify their actions and reactions. We must find a way to heal from the pain of rejection. The author discussed a five-dimensional healing process as a resolve to end this cycle: forgiveness, releasing, wholeness, restoration, and love.

God's word reminds us that Christ experienced rejection as he taught the gospel. He was rejected as the Messiah, the son of the Living God. While reading God's word, we also discover that the rejected stone, Christ, became the chief cornerstone, serving as the spiritual foundation for humanity. A cornerstone is laid at the corner of two walls to bind and strengthen them. In the bible, it symbolizes strength and significance. Today, the chief cornerstone is seated at the Father's right hand, interceding for us and awaiting his moment to rule and reign as King of Kings for all eternity.

How can we genuinely pursue our heart's desires if we do not know what God desires for us? Embracing His desires instills inner discipline, allowing us to prioritize the importance of people and situations that affect our decision-making. I discovered my identity in Christ when my desire for God surpassed anything else. I can also assure you that a personal relationship with Christ will never be one-sided. He will always fight for you and be a cover for those of us who are single. He will remain a source of stability when life attempts to shatter our hopes and dreams. Like the heart, Christ desires to become the center of our being. If you want to understand self-love and how to love others, He is our example.

Overcoming our heart matters is vital because it helps us to leave the pigpen. It was never intended to be our permanent dwelling place, fostering feelings of poor self-esteem, self-pity, failure, loneliness, and hopelessness. What a beautiful transformation! Eventually, you stop caring if you mix in with the fakes, losing the desire for superficial friendships. Allowing God to eliminate any lingering traces of the past restores your vision and sense of smell. Finally, opposition and disappointment can no longer anesthetize your ability to give and receive love freely.

I devoted much time and thought to writing this chapter of the book. Ladies, we are the heartbeat of our families. We reserve the right to wear the "S " on our chest because of our ability to multitask and apply our impressive problem-solving skills. We are the glue that holds everyone and everything together. Sometimes, I buy a gourmet cupcake, put a candle on it, and celebrate myself. This action is not a sign of arrogance but a small encouragement that I am valid and appreciated. The most crucial advice I can offer from this chapter to help you stay replenished is to guard your heart. Heart matters will consistently arise in various seasons of our lives, and we must learn how to effectively resolve them for personal growth and a sense of well-being.

Confession Moment Exercise

➢ List some people and things (good or bad) that can affect your heart.

➢ What are some heart matters that you need to confess and resolve?

➢ List some of your desires that you want to see come to fruition. List some proactive steps that will help you accomplish what you have written.

Scriptural Support Readings:

- ➤ Psalms 37:4: "Take delight in the Lord, and He will give you your heart's desires." [HCSB]

- ➤ Psalms 118:22: "The stone that the builders rejected has become the cornerstone." [HCSB]Matthew 6:21: "For where your treasure is, there your heart will be also." [HCSB]

- ➤ Mark 12:30: "Love the Lord your God with all your heart, with all your soul, with all our mind, and with all your strength." [HCSB]

- ➤ I Corinthians 13:4,5,6,7,8: "Love is patient, love is kind. Love does not envy, is not boastful, is not conceited, does not act improperly, is not selfish, is not provoked, and does not keep a record of wrongs. Love finds no joy in unrighteousness but rejoices in the truth. It bears all things, believes all things, hopes all things, endures all things." [HCSB]

- ➤ I Corinthians 13:13: "Now these three remain: faith, hope, and love. But the greatest of these is love." [HCSB]

- ➤ I John 4:8: "The one who does not love does not know God, because God is love." [HCSB]

- ➤ I Peter 4:8: "Above all, maintain an intense love for each other, since love covers a multitude of sins." [HCSB]

Chapter 6: Birthing Your Gifts

"A gift opens doors for a man and brings him before the great."

- Proverbs 18:16

What are gifts? Indeed, it is a fundamental question, but let us delve deeper beyond its general definition. God created man with spiritual and natural talents. God willingly gives both without payment. Gifts serve the purpose of glorifying the Father in Heaven and helping others. Examples of natural gifts include singing, writing, playing an instrument, and being a dominating athlete. Examples of spiritual gifts include teaching, encouraging, giving, and having words of wisdom and knowledge. One of God's greatest gifts created is you! You are a gift to those you meet and those close to you. Be the kind of gift that others are delighted to receive.

Some may ask how one can identify their talents and gifts. The answer to the question is simple. What are you good at doing? What are your strengths? Do you have one ability or talent, or do you have several? Ultimately, you should ask God, the creator, if you want to know what gifts you possess. Finally, reading and educating yourself on the types of spiritual gifts are equally important. These answers may seem basic, but as I worked to answer these same questions, it helped narrow my thoughts to focus on what I needed to spend time and energy pursuing.

Following these simple steps can assist you with making sound judgments. For example, suppose singing is not one of your talents. In that case, there is no need to traumatize the music director or judges as you are dismissed during auditions. This scenario reminds me of all the talent reality shows where individuals sign up and stand in line for hours to chase the wrong dream. Madness and disappointment arise when the judges give them a proper dose of honesty to inform them that singing or acting is not a talent to pursue. Yes, some do it for the few seconds of fame, but was it worth being reminded of five or ten years from now when someone replays or reminds them of that embarrassing moment they acted upon impulse and disregarded rational thinking?

My discovery of gifts unfolded with time. As I pursued my professional career, I began to delve into personal goals that helped identify some of my gifted areas. I remember going back to my college days when I would stay up the night before and effortlessly write essays to meet the assignment deadlines. This advantage allowed extra time to focus on more demanding areas like math and science.

During that time, I was not aware that my talents and spiritual gifts worked together. I embraced and utilized some gifts, while others remained untapped simply because I had not realized their potential due to a lack of vision and understanding. Today, I make a purposeful effort to use my gifts. I am always asking God to help me to identify other undiscovered gifts. Your gifts and talents will open the right doors of opportunity, making your goals and personal desires achievable. Using your gifts expands your territory and opens doors of opportunity that others may never imagine.

Gift Discovery Brings Reinvention!

At age thirty-nine, it was as if an explosive was ignited and broke the entrance to a blocked dam. Fresh, innovative ideas energized me to write again. I had to ask what triggered this new movement. I had come to a place of dormancy and was losing zeal to desire more of life. I had been questioning God for ten years about my reason for existing. Of course, I, too, had a purpose. While in a moment of prayer and meditation, I had come to that place of discovery.

I experienced a spiritual awakening moment, and my eyes opened to the call of destiny. Pictorial flashbacks flooded my mind, each piece fitting together like a puzzle. I saw how my gifts and talents had been perfected and intertwined as passion and purpose collided. I reached a place of knowledge to understand how they all played a part in who I am today. Not by my own will but because God knew I was willing to accept the call of purpose to perform His will. The next few years would bring testing to determine my commitment to the desires and aspirations I had been earnestly pursuing. Testing through training and preparation for the next dimension, becoming perfectly designed and ready for use from the refiner's fire. What adjustments will you make when your creator invites you to use your gifts?

I no longer identify myself as who I have become professionally. There is much more to share with others besides that area. As I take another look now, therein lies an author, a playwright, a song and content creator, a motivator, an educator, and a cultivator to the ingenious Millennial and Gen Z generations—one who assists with the process of journey discovery. To be a sounding board of wisdom, a gift they mostly lack due to age and inexperience, to steer their professional and personal zeal in the right direction to prevent wandering in the wilderness of life and pursuing the wrong things. What do you see as you look at who you have become? Is it favorable and productive, or should you remain in the refinery a little longer for clarity and instruction? Each elevation of life requires a training stage for perfection. If we desire evolution, the refinery will become a place of familiarity.

Reinvention will identify your flaws and cause you to fine-tune some areas. For example, a previous job challenged my skillset later in my career. The prior knowledge of specific skills I had been performing for the last fourteen years required change. If I wanted to advance myself, I had to transition to the new processes necessary to perform the job. My initial thoughts were to find another job. Indeed, this was not the industry standard, but I embraced the change soon after. I had to be willing to change to remain competitive and ahead of the curve. The words teachable and trainable were imperative to mastering this new task. I had to lay aside pride and embrace the fact that I had not reached the peak of my professional career. Initially, the progression was rocky, but stabilization came as I focused on the daily tasks and cleared my mind of the negative thoughts. I needed to remind myself that growth equals change.

Use your skills and talents to produce the vision of what you now see. Success and reinvention will not fall into your lap because of your giftedness. As previously stated, it opens the right doors, but prayer, planning, and strategy must accompany this new undertaking. From the moment we entered creation, man was introduced to a world full of possibilities. God desires to take our place of emptiness and fill it with greatness. It pleases Him immensely when we honor him by using our gifts to serve His purpose.

I cannot end this chapter without sharing the most incredible opportunity that could happen to us: the gift of salvation. Eternal salvation is received by placing our faith in Christ and confessing him as our Lord and Savior. Our salvation is secured through God's grace and obedience to His word. Some people are reluctant to receive gifts because they assume a hidden cost or stipulation must exist. I can say that both interpretations are false. It cannot be bought, and good deeds cannot acquire it. Christ's bloodshed and death on the cross were the costly price paid. There is nothing like a clean slate, and I can promise that Christ is waiting for an invitation to give you one. Whoever seeks to know His ways and do what He says will be blessed. It is up to us to decide how we want to spend our time on Earth. Upon recognizing the significance of the redemption being offered, I accepted it joyfully, and it has made an indelible impact on every aspect of my life. The gift of salvation is the one that I desire and purposefully intend to keep.

Birthing Your Gifts

Gifting Exercise

> ➢ Take a moment to assess your skills, abilities, and talents.

> ➢ Write them out on a piece of paper or in a journal, or become creative and create a vision board.

> ➢ Write a plan of how your gifts and talents can be used to serve someone else.

> ➢ Pray and ask God to help you identify any other gifts awaiting discovery.

- ➤ I Peter 4:10: "Based on the gift each one has received, use it to serve others, as good managers of the varied grace of God" [HCSB]

- ➤ Colossians 3:17: "And whatever you do, in word, or in deed, do everything in the name of the Lord Jesus, giving thanks to God the Father through Him" [HCSB]

- ➤ Matthew 25:15: "To one he gave five talents, to another, two; and to another, one- to each according to his own ability" [HCSB]

- ➤ Romans 10:9: "If you confess with your mouth, Jesus is Lord, and believe in your heart that God raised him from the dead, you will be saved." [HCSB]

- ➤ Daniel 2:22: "He reveals the deep and hidden things; He knows what is in the darkness, and light dwells with him" [HCSB

Chapter 7: Operating In Wisdom

"Now if any of you lacks wisdom, he should ask God, who gives to all generously and without criticizing, and it will be given to him."

- *James 1:5*

God wants us to be knowledgeable, disciplined, and wise. If you lack wisdom, seek guidance from the Holy Spirit. Knowledge helps us apply what we have learned or act upon what we have heard. Learning is essential if we are to advance and acquire new perspectives. Once again, we must be teachable. I had to revisit this lesson while editing the book when a peer challenged me to improve my calling.

While growing up, I used to hear that girls were "sassy," there was a brief period when I fit that description. I had to have the last remark in the disagreement. Unfortunately, this unacceptable behavior was short-lived once I discovered that my immaturity only hurt me. Others did not value my opinion even when it was good advice. Furthermore, I did not have enough life experience to advise others or interject my opinions on specific topics. I soon learned that having the last word did not matter. I was not too fond of the appearance of being immature and undisciplined. Our remarks should positively influence the person we communicate with, so make sure your words have meaning. Younger generations have not mastered this insight. I remind them to carefully choose their words, be mindful of their tone, and consider their expressions. Their communication with others could shatter relationships or open doors of opportunity.

Parents, please address inappropriate communication and behavior to prevent your child from facing unnecessary rejection. Others with standards will not tolerate immature conduct. Parenting continues into adulthood and must also trump being our child's friend. Everyone needs accountability! If we do not teach them, life will. Life can be a harsh teacher and does not consider your emotions.

Our world is different than when we were teenagers and young adults, yet our parents' old-fashioned ideals can be just as successful with our kids. I know this to be true as I observe my friends raise their teens and young adults. It is a tug of war at times, but the adults always prevail. They were also instilled with strong morals early on, imparting those standards to their children. Individuals must make wise selections, and as parents, we must lead by Godly example, both privately and publicly.

Today, I still follow the guidance of my mom and mentors. Growing in wisdom as we age is highly desirable, and selecting the right mentor is essential. My first step in choosing a mentor begins with identifying someone who practices what they teach. I am not interested in the "Do as I say and not as I do" mentality. Offering valuable advice does not automatically make someone a mentor or life coach.

Wisdom reduces tolerance for immoral behavior and speech. Another person can drive you to greater heights or hold you back with negative words or actions. Surround yourself with good, ambitious people who will challenge your thinking and living. Seek the support of those who motivate you to accomplish your goals. You cannot fly with eagles if you chase and mingle with chickens. Chickens have limited flying ability, while eagles boast a wingspan three times that of a chicken, and night blindness makes them vulnerable to predators. A chicken is unattractive, but an eagle soars and glides gracefully across the open skies. Its eyesight is sharp and engaging, only descending low to catch prey.

My grandmother used to raise chickens in a coop without a roof. The chickens would fly out and graze in the yard but were easily lured back into the coop with food. I am not implying that chickens are "bad people." They have a limited outlook and lack a broad mindset. A good friend once said you cannot expect friendship qualities from projects. All things must have a proper placeholder. You must know those individuals you are assigned to help versus those aligned with your destiny.

Wisdom aids in spiritual and physical growth. Life lessons play a crucial role in personal maturity, especially regarding letting go of past hurts and failures. Moving forward is difficult if you are focused on yesterday's cares. It is not logical to remain at rest and move forward simultaneously, as the Law of Motion dictates that we move one way or another. Forgiving oneself and others is a necessary step for spiritual and emotional healing. Forgiving others is a requirement if we want the Heavenly Father to forgive us.

Let us briefly discuss the importance of having wisdom. Wisdom brings financial freedom in the form of wealth. King Solomon is noted in the bible as the richest and wisest king. Solomon discovered the key to obtaining wealth was to attain the knowledge and wisdom of God. He was young when he inherited the throne and lacked leadership experience. Solomon could have asked for riches, long life, or the death of his enemies, but he chose differently when God asked him what he desired. Instead, he asked God for an obedient heart to rule justly and to discern between good and evil. God was pleased with Solomon's request. He not only gave Solomon what he asked for but also gave him riches, wealth, and honor, so much so that no other man in any kingdom would compare. Solomon also received wisdom and strategy concerning construction (the building of Solomon's temple), the contribution of trade routes, and the gift of becoming a literary scholar. These achievements are a few examples of what he was able to accomplish.

Securing financial wealth is a wise decision. Money is a requirement to make things happen. God's word states that it is the answer to everything. The problem arises when the love of money and power minimizes the importance of wisdom. Compromising one's morality and character, spawning corruption and evil, thus bringing dishonor to the one who allowed you to obtain it.

Sadly, some individuals in today's world misuse financial influence to control others. "What shall it profit a man to gain the entire world and lose his soul eternally?" The bible's instruction is the compass for managing wealth. Humility and humbleness serve as guiding principles as we navigate life's journey. Some of my most remarkable journeys were approached with humility.

Also, as believers in Christ, our primary focus should remain on those things that are eternal. The gift of eternal life is the ultimate treasure. Solomon possessed wisdom, intellect, wealth, influence, and power, yet he concluded that all these things were futile. He compelled man to fear God and follow His commandments.

Speaking of direction, let me give you this thought to consider. It defies logic to travel downward to receive something extraordinary, as "Up" is always known as the better alternative. Pursuing that which is beneath or hidden can seem invaluable. In the bible, the remnant of a king's lineage was concealed in a lowly place (Lo-debar). Upon discovery, the royal was given his grandfather's inheritance. He became an honored member of the royal house of Solomon's father, the great King David. Who would pass on the opportunity to meet and connect with royalty? Dark and lowly places can conceal hidden treasures. Carefully consider those opportunities that are affirmed but seem undesirable. I humbly admit I have missed open doors of opportunity (destiny doors). The gift of God's wisdom is essential to responding to life's situations. Adhere to God's wisdom instead of man's wisdom and understanding. Again, as believers in Christ, we must have faith, as God's capabilities are endless.

I distinctly remember a season where it seemed like I was losing due to taking the risk. God showed up in the last minute of my darkest hour and reassured me that his infinite wisdom never fails. He intended a clear victory for me, even when it seemed impossible. During that season of my life, I experienced a series of resurrections in various forms, but it required me to take the leap and risk it all.

I have already discussed in previous chapters the opposition I faced while writing this book. A breaking point came a few years ago when I was confident the book was finished. Finally, I reached the end of completion. I overcame the labor pains of losing sleep by rising early to research and write. My baby would soon become a tangible product.

Continuous problems arose during various phases of trying to complete the book. Due to circumstances beyond my control, I could not proceed with this project. This led to feelings of frustration and confusion, causing me to pause. Attempting to finish this book eventually left me exhausted. Other areas in my life were equally demanding my time and attention, forcing me to walk away. Months later, I proceeded to converse with God to remind Him of His spoken words concerning this assignment and that I originally had no desire to write a book. My only desire was to be obedient and to yield to what was uncontrollably yearning in my spirit.

I felt a stillbirth occurring, so I humbled myself and asked God for clarity. Without hesitation, I received an apparent response to what was happening. First, I had to prioritize the tasks I was working on. Secondly, I needed to work steadily instead of rushing to produce this product. Most importantly, the book served as the launching pad and groundwork for the vision I received in building my brand. A solid foundation is crucial for what is being constructed on top of it. It had to be established on God's word, and I needed a deeper understanding. Cultivating others requires discipline to study. What sane person would allow someone to diagnose or perform an operation on them without knowing if the physician or surgeon obtained the education and specific credentials to do so? It was necessary to "tie" my hands to slow the process due to the significance of the work.

God had not forgotten his promise. I had to wait for the correct time to publish the book, but I could not do it until I "studied to show myself approved" so I would not be ashamed. I also had to deal with some heart matters that surfaced during this process to give an unbiased account of the life lessons and experiences I am sharing with you. Purpose demonstrates your commitment to God and reveals areas for spiritual growth. Today, I am still learning the value of discipline.

God extends His grace and patience towards us so we may learn to do the same for others. Indeed, it is a humbling experience when He brings our lives full circle. The very thing we walk away from is what He calls us back to complete. Before I could turn the page to begin a new chapter, I had to submit once more and re-enter the refinery. Who knows the ways of the Lord? He will transition you from a lowly desert to settle you in a wealthy place. "Blessed is the one who trusts in the Lord." "Blessed are those who desire to understand and delight in His ways, as his ways are merciful and righteous."

"For His thoughts are higher than your thoughts." "He will lift you up with His righteous right hand."

God will grant the request to grow in wisdom and grace if we desire it. There are moments where my growth happens quickly, requiring my full attention. Growth in various aspects of my life is a continuous process. Time, experience, heeding the words of wisdom from the older generation, and receiving the gift of Godly counsel contribute to this growth. The wisdom passed down from older generations offers a wealth of knowledge as they have lived through many of life's lessons. The significance of exercising wisdom as you age and advance in life cannot be overstated. Please recognize the power of wisdom; it can be the key to unlocking a fulfilling and successful life.

In my youth, I saw my mom as a buzzkill. No one could have fun or live recklessly when she was around. However, as I have gotten older, I realize she only safeguarded the precious thing she cherished and would unquestionably sacrifice her life to protect. Now that I am a mother, I can relate directly to her feelings and understand her actions. Learning this lesson has been a humbling experience for me as I watch my son with his children.

Take advantage of this opportunity to read, contemplate, and engage in the exercises presented in this book. I dedicated hours to prayer before and during the assignment of writing these words onto the pages of this book. I strive to reflect Christ. I asked for the knowledge and understanding of what to share with His daughters. If you seek the answers, He will surely provide them. He eagerly awaits us to ask, and it pleases Him immensely when we follow His instructions with a heart of gratitude.

Reflection Exercise

➢ Reflect on some of your life-altering moments where you exercised the gift of wisdom to make informed decisions that produced a positive outcome.

➢ What other areas of opportunity are you interested in pursuing that require strategic wisdom, planning, and guidance? Write out a plan of execution for those opportunities.

- Proverbs 4:6,7: "Do not forsake wisdom, and she will protect you; love her, and she will watch over you. Wisdom is supreme-so gotten wisdom. And whatever else you get, get understanding." HCSB

- Proverbs 9:10: "The fear of the Lord is the beginning of wisdom, and the knowledge of the Holy One is understanding." [HCSB]

- Proverbs 19:20- "Listen to counsel and receive instruction so that you may be wise later in life." [HCSB]

- Proverbs 10:22: "The Lord's blessing enriches, and struggle adds nothing to it." [HCSB]

- Ecclesiastes 10:19: "A feast is prepared for laughter, and wine makes life happy, and money is the answer for everything." [HCSB]

- Proverbs 14:1: "Every wise woman builds her house, but a foolish one tears it down with her own hands." [HCSB]

Chapter 8: God's Promises

- *Luke 18:27*

Indeed, promises are a common part of human interactions. Whether promises are made by parents, spouses, friends, bosses, or leaders, we encounter them in various aspects of our lives. While human intentions are often sincere, promises may be broken for many reasons. On the contrary, God operates differently. His abundant promises are His intended plans to bless our future, and you can discover them in His word. Be open to the various channels He uses to communicate them to you. These divine intentions benefit not only us but also those connected to us. We will see this statement demonstrated later in the chapter.

Dreaming, praying, studying, and meditating are some ways I receive communication from God. Reading His word daily also helps to keep my mind renewed. Some days pose a challenge to be diligent, but I recognize its necessity. I need this intimate time alone with my creator, and I urge you to do the same. Making time for yourself in the early morning can have a powerful impact on the rest of your day. During this time, I often receive clarity and guidance for direction to keep me focused.

Gaining clarity and direction also aids in avoiding the temptation to resort to a Plan B while waiting for a promise. He has already written the complete story. Yes, He allows us to exercise free will, but this fundamental ability to make choices is a gift that should not be taken lightly. Choosing Plan B may result in settling for permissive desires, missing out on God's perfect blessings. Therefore, embracing our free will with responsibility and wisdom is imperative.

Being in God's divine will is always better, even if it means waiting. Let us turn our weary moments into powerful moments of prayer so that we may resist the urge to take shortcuts on our journey toward our dreams. By relying on prayer for guidance, we can find the strength, courage, and determination to overcome any obstacle and achieve our goals with grace and perseverance. This practice also strengthens my faith to confidently believe that God will conclude the matter. Even if He chooses to write a new chapter, I still have an assurance of receiving the promise.

Whatever God promised, you can rest assured that it will be fulfilled. He never breaks the covenants he establishes with man. God's words to Noah serve as a powerful example of an unconditional promise. He made a three-part covenant with him:

1. Destruction by flood will never occur on the earth again.

2. The seasons will always come as expected as long as the earth remains.

3. A rainbow's visibility during rain will signify to man that God is faithful to keep his promise.

The enduring presence of these three everlasting covenants is a powerful testament to God's infinite love and boundless compassion for all of His creation.

Have you ever made plans based on a promise, only to find out things didn't go as expected? Do not worry; you are not alone in this. I once held onto a promise, confident that it would come true, only to realize it was not meant to be at that moment. It is funny how life works. We briefly discussed this topic in a previous chapter, but its importance brings me back to the subject to elaborate on my earlier question.

Many of us aspire to be a wife and have our own family. Approaching the end of my thirties, I decided to forego the possibility of marriage if it did not occur by my early forties.

The idea of sharing my life with another daily, mainly when I was accustomed to providing for myself, required significant adjustment. I was losing sight of God's promise of marriage, which was spoken ten years prior. His promise was not to be someone's girlfriend, a friend with benefits, or a life destined to singleness, but to be a wife, a help meet.

I had a life moment with myself and concluded, why give up on the promise, and why settle for Jacob when I could wait on the transformation of Israel? For those who need to become more familiar with the story, I highly recommend reading the books of Genesis and Hosea. Jacob was a highly strategic individual with a splendid work ethic, but his integrity was questionable.

He fled for his life from his brother Esau after his father had unknowingly given Jacob his brother's birthright. Guided by his mother's instructions, Jacob sought shelter with his uncle Laban, who later became his father-in-law. Eventually, conflicts arose between them as Laban lacked integrity as well. After serving Laban for twenty years, Jacob, now prosperous, took his household and livestock and headed back for his homeland, Canaan, without informing Laban. Laban was displeased with this decision and unsuccessfully proceeded to stop him from reaching his destination. Lastly, Jacob's favoritism towards his son Joseph triggered jealousy and resentment among his brothers. Some of his sons also inherited some unfavorable characteristics.

While reading, I was reminded of the expression, "Be careful of what you ask for." I always admired the part of the story about how Jacob loved Rachel. It would be nice to experience that kind of love. Surely, I only gave thought to some of the story. Jacob willingly served Laban for seven years to marry Rachel, unaware he would be tricked into marrying Laban's first daughter, Leah. Jacob had to serve Laban an additional seven years to wed Rachel. Leah was a lingering, permanent shadow in their lives, and Jacob did not love her. Unfortunately, she was not going anywhere.

As I explored the life of the man formerly known as Jacob, I concluded that he was not what I desired at all. It became evident that change was also necessary for me to receive God's promises. I, too, was lacking wholeness. When you ask God for something, be clear about your desire. Is it integral? What are its qualities and attributes? If it does not align with your vision, will you wait for it to mature? Do you need to mature in certain areas as well? I would have cheated myself had I cashed in and settled for Jacob. I would have been sorely disappointed a couple of years later upon realizing that what I took at face value was worth far less than what was initially presented. I could have easily argued that I was beguiled, but truthfully, I misled myself by letting my emotions guide my choices instead of listening to my inner voice. At some point, we must decide never to go back to the Pigpen.

I have encountered a few Jacobs, but I did not want a lifetime commitment with someone unsure of their identity or purpose. While they were great providers, there were better suitors to help me fulfill my purpose. I aspire to be with someone capable of speaking encouraging words in challenging times and praying for me when situations seem unfavorable. I do not want to sound redundant, but it is imperative to understand your identity in Christ and acknowledge the qualities you possess.

Jacob's name was changed to Israel in the story after he tenaciously wrestled with God and triumphed, so God blessed him. In addition, Jacob had a promise from God, the same promise made to his father, Isaac, and grandfather, Abraham. This significant divine encounter changed his character and life journey as he trusted God, influencing how he would navigate his plans. A meaningful change was necessary for him and his family, and he was willing to take a risk. He was returning home and needed to make amends with his brother Esau. Jacob had too much at stake not to use wisdom.

Jacob had gained two wives and thirteen children since the last time he laid eyes on Canaan. Also, twenty years of labor as a herder proved successful. These occurrences called for a different response. Jacob was now ready to receive God's promise and join the ranks of his father and grandfather. The promises of land, the promise of descendants, and to be a blessing to all nations were fulfilled. Birthed from his lineage are The Twelve tribes of Judah.

Do not forfeit your promise due to discouragement. Persevere through the obstacle until it remains no more. We must be bold and prayerful like Jacob. He was unsure if Esau would receive him and his family; nevertheless, he persisted. It was a sobering moment for Jacob when his brother passionately embraced him. I can imagine Jacob's overwhelming feelings of gratitude and relief. You and I can experience those same emotions as we enter the door to our promised land. Witnessing the tangible fulfillment of the promise relieves all doubt, affirming God as a faithful promise keeper.

The long anticipation of a promise makes the heart weary. The promising news triggers your curiosity for the details about how, where, and when. In today's fast-paced world, we often desire instant fulfillment of promises, even when we know that we cannot manage them if they were given to us that way. We would crush under pressure to maintain what was given. What we once desired quickly begins to change our mindset. Recalling the promise in your mind is accurate in what you are to receive, but the timing did not align with God's. Consequently, we are willing to walk away from what should have been God's perfect will for us.

Patience is not an area to be desired while learning the value of waiting. When promises do not align with our present reality, impatience may push us to take matters into our own hands. Faith can waver, and we shift ourselves into the driver's seat. Waiting is a bittersweet subject as I reflect on past losses or made a mess of situations when I moved prematurely. Let me reassure you that God does not require our assistance to fulfill His promise to us. However, He does expect us to do our part. We must understand what is expected of us regarding God's promises.

Promises are also conditional, which means that our involvement is needed. Faith requires action. Take Jacob, for instance; he worked fourteen years for his father-in-law to receive Rachel. He was willing to work for what he desired to have. That was quite a long time to wait on a promise, yet he remained faithful to his agreement with Laban.

Being productive while waiting for God's promises to manifest helps to rid the feelings of anxiousness and doubt. Stay focused and committed to purpose instead of the promise. The busyness of purpose will keep you occupied until the promise comes. Let me give you another relatable example. Have you ever undertaken a time-consuming project? The day starts, and you find yourself working through lunch. The afternoon hits, and it is time to wrap up the workday. Fast-forward to Friday afternoon, and your mind is trying to process the week's events. Time becomes a non-factor as your focus shifts to completing the assignment. Weeks roll by, and you reach the end of the project, witnessing the outcome of dedicated hard work. Receiving a promise from God is just as rewarding as seeing the project's outcome. Stay committed to your promise, and soon it will become a reality.

Receiving just one promise from God can outweigh any perceived losses. If we wait, God's compensation will far exceed our expectations. This leads me to share another personal yet encouraging life experience of those wonderful plans I made for myself. Have faith if you cannot conceive. "Believe in the possibility of having the child you have been waiting for, even when it seems impossible." Be open to adoption and other viable routes to motherhood. You see, I thought that I would experience childbirth, but God had other plans for me concerning motherhood. Instead of trusting Him when those plans did not unfold, I lost hope and was unhappy with God for several years because I had not been blessed with the one thing I desired most. I limited God's capability, thinking he would bless me by conceiving, only to discover His plan was far greater.

I am grateful to God for blessing me with a wonderful nephew whom I raised as a son since the tender age of one, and not once has he caused me any heartache or pain. I could not have asked for a more perfect gift. In addition, my son has gifted me with three unique grandchildren and a talented, nurturing daughter-in-law. My life now is truly full. At this moment, I am tearful as I share this experience with you. Only

God helped me understand that he indeed granted my heart's desire. He made me a mother before I could even ask, which has been the most beautiful and humbling experience.

Surprisingly, my purpose has called me to be a mother to many individuals. Had I had my own child, it would have been a challenge financially and mentally to raise many others within my family and extended family. God has truly kept His promise to make me a mother, and I would have missed the revelation of being a mother had God not revealed this to me at the right time.

God, our heavenly father's precision of time is impeccable, and we, as parents, strive to operate in the same manner concerning our children. We would never allow our five-year-old to sit behind the wheel of our car to take us anywhere. We only release that kind of trust and authority to them when they have reached the age of maturity to handle that kind of responsibility. Do not allow time and circumstances to dim your hope. Trust in His word and have faith. God has not forgotten you! When obedience and timing align, you will receive the promises of God.

➤ List a few promises that you have already received.

➤ List the promises that you are still waiting to see manifest. Now, add a couple of scriptures listed at the end of this chapter or a couple that will build your faith. Reminding God of what has been promised to you according to His word is entirely acceptable.

➤ Find a trusted person, ask them to support you in your goals, and hold you accountable.

"If God has performed it once, He is faithful to perform it again."

- Isaiah 40:21: "But those who trust in the Lord shall renew their strength; they will soar on wings like eagles; they will run and not grow weary; they will walk and not faint." [HCSB]

- Mark 11:24: "Therefore I tell you, all the things you pray and ask for-believe that you have received them, and you will have them." [HCSB]

- Philippians 4:6: "Don't worry about anything, but in everything, through prayer and petition with thanksgiving, let your requests be made known to God." [HCSB]

- Philippians 4:19,20: "And my God will supply all your needs according to His riches in glory in Christ Jesus. Now to our God and Father be glory forever and ever. Amen." [HCSB]

- James 1:2,3,4: "Consider it a great joy my brothers, whenever you experience various trails, knowing that the testing of your faith produces endurance. But endurance must do its complete work, so that you may be mature and complete, lacking nothing." [HCSB]

- Jeremiah 1:12: "The Lord said to me, "You have seen correctly, for I watch over my word to accomplish it." [HCSB]

➢ Hebrews 10:23: "Let us hold on to the confession of our hope without wavering, for He who promised is faithful." [HCSB]

➢ 2 Peter 3:9: "The Lord does not delay his promise, as some understand delay, but is patient with you, not wanting any to perish but all to come to repentance." [HCSB]

In Closing...

Discovering your purpose begins with asking the one who created you. God is waiting for an invitation to share and reveal more about you. Knowing who you are helps to avoid an identity crisis. Our physical nature often guides us to adopt worldly perspectives, hindering our spiritual growth. As we advance, let us try to prevent that from happening.

Speaking of advancing, you may become temporarily unavailable while preparing for the next chapter of life. Your purpose may require your undivided attention. Do not change your position if others complain that you are inaccessible. Esther's family could not visit her during her time of preparation. She was busy preparing for her new future role. Mordecai would walk the palace courtyard near the harem daily to hear any news on Esther's progress. Eventually, the day finally arrived to reveal her progress, and that day will also come for you. You and those closest to you are excited to celebrate your accomplishments. In Esther's case, she became queen, and everyone in the kingdom knew her name, as the king held a banquet in her honor. Remain hopeful during this process because the very thing seeking to share what you have discovered will find you. Waiting can be challenging, but wisdom enables you to withhold until the right time.

The lessons I learned while preparing also brought advancement and transformation. The first lesson guided me toward gaining self-confidence, accountability, and maturity. Secondly, mind transformation helped me to deal with the issues that tagged themselves to my past. Pursuing purpose will force you to stand face forward with opposition, and stand in your truth, no matter how it makes you feel or how others may feel.

Next, I needed to gain control of my emotions. This was an important area that I needed to address. During this time, I experienced joy, astonishment, fear, rejection, disappointment, and lastly, complete peace. I began to pen again once I experienced peace. I was no longer writing from a place of pain but a place of deliverance. Being free from sickness and the roller coaster of emotions was a liberating experience. The sting of rejection eventually became a momentary sore spot, and now memories of the past. God is the source of healing our inner being, and His word is the ultimate source of truth. When your inner sustenance is filled with God's word, honesty and truth override the negative emotions that arise. Honesty and truth are arsenal tools that defeat the mind's battles against you. You will always remain defeated if you do not use the correct warfare tools. It is foolish to take a knife to a gunfight.

Transformation of the new Alean also allowed me to see past my façade to expose what was lying underneath. I needed to destroy the barriers of my secret internal hauntings and deal with my brokenness. The state of brokenness has the potential to weaken your zeal and passion for purpose or lead to a lack of desire to understand why you were created. It can also draw other broken people into your circle. God's healing from brokenness is crucial because it is difficult to help others when you are hurt. Well, let me speak for myself. During my season of brokenness, my will to settle took precedence. Joining others in their place of unhappiness felt natural because that experience was relatable. This is why believers in Christ cannot linger in that state. A transformed mind was my escape from this rabbit hole of despair.

I received healing in this area by permitting myself to heal from the broken places of my life by submerging myself in the promises of God and His word. There is a scripture in God's word for the challenges I face. Once I received healing, I passionately pursued wholeness. Wholeness will allow you to believe again in God's promises. There is unexplainable freedom in healing and wholeness. Wholeness attracts the experience of being pursued by a suitable mate, the right job, or any other situation with a right to attach itself to you and your destiny.

A spiritual awakening transpired in this season as well. Broken were the chains of religious tradition. I relied on the Holy Spirit to teach me "all things" concerning my salvation. Freedom in this area became as essential as the need to breathe. The more I relied on the Holy Spirit, the stronger the craving became to experience God in a whole new way. Banished to return no more was the chicken mindset. This eagle was willing to stretch her wingspan at maximum capacity to soar because she experienced the true essence of freedom.

God placed in my path true teachers of The Gospel. They are helping me understand God's kingdom commands and instructions. I have experienced acceleration in my relationship with Christ, which has elevated me to a whole new dimension. This has been a life-changing experience for me, and I am grateful for the immense blessings that have come with it. "Whom the son sets free is free indeed."

Encountering wholeness increased my confidence in the changed version of myself despite past opinions. My good friend and life coach's words became engraved in my thoughts. She stressed that baggage is a destroyer, and we must lighten our load to remain mobile to help others do the same. I had to listen and heed the words of wisdom, for wisdom accelerates growth.

Esther experienced a growth process as well. She was pampered, trained, and cultivated by one of the king's most trustworthy servants before she could become queen. Esther's royal preparation took twelve months, prompting me to pause and ask the question during my journey, "When did my transition occur?" My transition happened when I decided to accept and respond to what God spoke to Alean concerning her identity. The process required preparation.

Likewise, I had to become willing to allow God to develop me so that I could mature and take my position as royalty. Patience, discipline, commitment, obedience, strategic guidance, constant communication with the Father through prayer, using my gifts, operating in faith, and resting in the assurance of His promises were all part of the training process. Hard work will eventually produce positive results, so expect to receive great rewards. God will train and cultivate you according to the level of your capacity for greatness. The greater the destiny assignment, the greater the intensity of training. I define greatness as accomplishing what you are supposed to do by fulfilling your God-given assignments. God gives us gifts and talents to complete those assignments; he has no favorites. Our response to how and what we pursue and our obedience to the instructions in His word sets us apart.

Lastly, I purchased a full-length mirror before the end of this process. I was never satisfied with my physical appearance. My negative self-view would steal those joyous moments of feeling empowered and beautiful. I have experienced cruel moments that made me withdraw from many opportunities that would have displayed my intellect. I am sure that after reading this section, most of my friends and family will be in shock because I never portrayed any signs of insecurity or weakness. I wore a powerful mask that hid any moments of doubt to let anyone believe that Alean was insecure about anything.

Maintaining a healthy weight has been a challenge for me since childhood, and I have experienced body shaming personally and in the professional arena. Although I lost considerable weight in the past fourteen years, I experienced a rapid gain in the last two years. The stressors of life can trigger areas you thought you had conquered. This regression was hard to accept, and I felt myself slipping back into unhealthy eating habits. Fortunately, I met a physician who saved my life and helped me get back on my journey of living. He rescued me from the thought of giving up by ministering to me spiritually. He also put me on a weight loss regimen that worked as a tool to help me lose and maintain my weight loss. I am so grateful to have found a physician who is concerned about my overall well-being. After forty-eight years, I have acknowledged that overcoming the weight challenge is a marathon, not a sprint. Living a healthy lifestyle has to be a life-long process.

I faced the mirror to agree with myself to love and accept the true me, regardless of how my outer being would transform going forward. If I were not pleased with what I saw, I would take proactive measures instead of convincing myself that I was satisfied with what I disliked externally. The days of covering my true feelings with make-up and trendy clothing had to end. My outer being must align and agree with my inner transformation. Sharing this moment with you is paramount; again, truthfulness brings freedom. While we are having this truth moment, let me assure you that everyone has some area of their life that is a constant battle of struggle. Please believe that your inner nemesis is no worse than the next person attempting to amplify your shortcomings. Their flaws and imperfections illuminate as much as yours when they become temporarily unguarded. So, when the person tries to remind you of your area of lack in those moments, it is appropriate to inform them that Christ was the only example of perfection, personified in the flesh.

Some of you may ask, "Now what?" as we close this chapter. Prayerfully, working through the exercises and meditating on the chapter topics will help you on your current path. However, God's divine purpose for you will present itself if you are genuinely seeking, and His plan will continue to unfold as you step toward His guidance. I know this to be true because God is continuously unfolding His plans for me as I speak to you in this book. Eight years have now passed since I began to write my journey. Releasing this work during this season was challenging, and I questioned if the material was still relevant. I have far surpassed where I began. I also lost my desire to finish this work a few years ago due to opposition.

At a moment's notice, God can rekindle your passion for purpose. He awakened this sleeping giant from its dormancy.

Destiny and purpose flowed forth like a refreshing well once more, and finishing the book became a priority. God revealed to Alean that her timing was not his timing. Although years have passed, completing this assignment and receiving this promise remained aligned with destiny. It was selfish to think that the book was written to benefit Alean. This book is for others and to help them through their journey of discovery. As I reflect, writing and reading my story is just as insightful for me as the next person needing to hear it. Purpose brings revelation and clarity, which God only reveals.

Our testimonies and the testimonies of others help us to overcome life's trials and obstacles. God shows his grace, reveals His power, and expresses love toward us during our trials. Within this work, I have shared testimonies of my trials and successes, and with God's help, I emerged victorious in each. God will also send someone to be a testament to your journey. Two friends, in particular, witnessed my growth from the initiation through the uncomfortable contractions, labor, and, finally, the birthing. Not only did he restore my life, but he also gave me a new one. Therefore, I am obliged to "lay down my life for him."

I want to leave with you one final wisdom nugget. "Enjoy the journey while on your road of destiny." Yes, every single moment! Initially, I had become fixated on the destination instead of enjoying the process. I could not see the victories or the accelerated growth. I pushed myself to a point where I experienced burnout. I have mentioned balance multiple times throughout this book due to its importance. Self-care is vital and needs to become a part of our everyday routine. Reflecting on my past, I can see the significant and small victories.

Why settle for less when you were pre-destined to conquer, as did Esther, and to soar graciously like an eagle? Woman, you are a beautifully designed masterpiece. Handcrafted and chosen by the creator to perform great exploits with what he has gifted you. An original masterpiece is well sought after and admired by the most prestigious of those who love that particular work of art. Anyone can purchase a copy or duplication of an original. They sell cheaply for affordability to the masses. It would be disheartening if the Father's authentic design piece remained hidden and unveiled. When your talents and moments of brilliance remain concealed, the only thing that others can see is a replica of someone else. God desires to have replicas of His son so the light of His truth may be revealed through us.

Let us remember the primary purpose of our reason to exist: to worship our Father and Creator. Everything that we do in life should exemplify His glory. Whether saving a race of people like Esther or saving those in your home, be the best at whatever you are assigned to do. If you sincerely try, you will flourish beyond your expectations and what others could not perceive concerning you. Pursuing destiny will ignite a flame for your true passion, and the only thing that others can see is a trail of the blazing fire of God's glory. Let Him seat you in the royal places of opportunity, confirming your right to wear the crown. Perhaps you are being chosen "for such a time as this!" Destiny is calling. How will you respond?

Nine Key Takeaways

- ❖ Love- Christ, the center of our being, is the answer to overcoming all heart matters!

- ❖ Disappointments- Do not despise disappointments; Allow disappointments to become seeds for growth!

- ❖ What you do versus who you are- Never let what you do take the driver's seat of who you are; balance is key. Until you discover who you are, what you do will continue to be your driving force!

- ❖ Opposition- Unbelief, fear, and rejection are destiny destroyers; Faith has the power to defeat all destiny destroyers!

- ❖ Wisdom, knowledge, and understanding are essential for maturity and growth!

- ❖ Be a gift while discovering your gifts!

- ❖ Vision brings your lens into focus!

- ❖ Mind over what Matters!

- ❖ Purpose has "Purpose"- Discover and complete what you were born to do!

Part Two

For Teen Girls

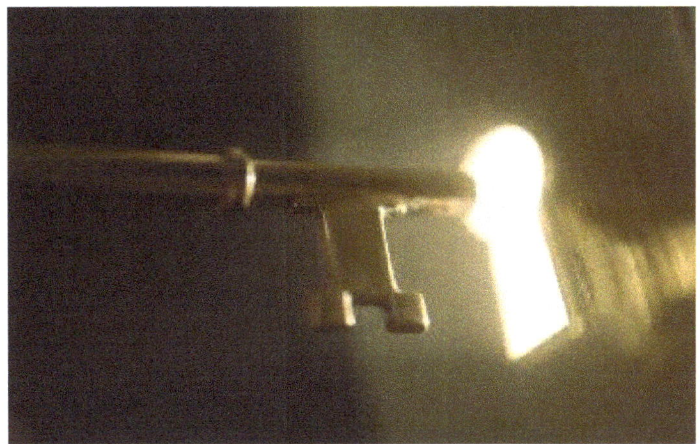

Has anyone ever purchased a journal for you with a keylock, or do you own a school locker? What is the purpose of the key, and are you securing it in a safe place so it would not get lost? These are simple questions, but I want you to consider them momentarily. Keys are essential, as they allow us to access and secure valuable things.

Picture driving your car to school, and as you leave for lunch, you discover your keys are missing. The key ring holds keys to your car, home, and locker. In that moment, you are clueless and traumatized due to the loss of something valuable. You search aimlessly, hoping no one has taken your keys because the last thing you want to do is call Mom to inform her that someone has stolen the car. Can you imagine losing the ability to drive your car again?

This scenario may seem extreme, but I want you to understand its importance. Just as you value the tangible things in life, I need you to see your future as being equally valuable. Each of us has a destiny to fulfill, and the key to achievement is already in our possession. We only need an understanding and the motivation to pursue it. This key must be safeguarded and entrusted to no one else, as it holds our future.

God is our source of discovering who we are. He is the engineer of our ability to think, make decisions, and gain the knowledge necessary to accomplish what we are predestined to do. So, let us use our master key to open the door to destiny and venture on a short journey into understanding who we are. Are you ready? Let's go!

Chapter 1: Who Am I? Discovering My Purpose!

Now that you have come into adolescence, I am sure you are discovering and experiencing many new things concerning yourself. Your likes and dislikes, attitudes and emotions, hormones, make-up, hair, hobbies, establishing friendships, driving for the first time, etcetera. What an exciting time for you! Exposure to life's events will influence who you become. This time should also be joyous and adventurous. You will only experience your teenage years once.

I can imagine you looking forward to enjoying your sweet sixteen celebrations, prom, senior photos, Grad Nite, and graduation. Each event is memorable and special, and your parents sacrifice to ensure you have the best memories of these moments. Remember to express your appreciation to them for making these moments possible. You are not entitled to attend these events, but your parents love you and want you to have the best experience.

While you are on this road of discovery, I encourage you to make intelligent decisions. Life choices have consequences, good or bad. It is crucial to listen to your parents and other adults as they guide you in the right direction. Spoiler alert! Whatever you and your friends do in secrecy is nothing new and probably has been done already.

Just ask someone older, and they can help you understand this truth.

Teenage years produce the mindset of believing you have all the correct answers because your parents' perspectives and views are outdated in today's society. Deciding what is best for you without guidance can lead to poor choices and costly mistakes. You find yourself in a losing battle with your parents, who understand the consequences based on experience. Even now, at my current age, I still seek guidance from my mom and other responsible adults when I face important decisions. Adulthood does not exclude us from learning and growing.

As parents and mentors, we want you to enjoy the advantages of what life offers, but it is important to express your thoughts positively. Your words and actions should always positively influence yourself and others. Will you make mistakes along the way? Absolutely, and that is okay. We will be here to pick you up when you stumble from the mistakes so you can move forward.

The world eagerly awaits your passion and creative thinking. I like to refer to Generation Z as "Forward Thinkers." Your generation has embraced innovative technology, and you are unafraid to take risks or speak out against social injustices. I have also witnessed in your generation the desire to be entrepreneurs. I have a few family members who are young business owners, and it is very admirable to watch them evolve. You are the generation who will bring the necessary change to improve our world.

<u>What Is Purpose?</u>

Purpose is "the reason for which something is done or for which something exists." If you have not asked yourself who you are and why you exist, I need you to stop and think about it for a moment. You did not end up in this adventurous world solely because your parents thought it would be a good idea. God created you with a purpose. He needed someone special to complete a specific task he had in mind, and he chose you. You are unique, and no one else can accomplish what you were created to do.

You will notice distinct differences if you compare your appearance to someone else. Even twins have specific traits that set them apart from each other. My family has a set of triplets (two girls and one boy). Although the two girls share a strong resemblance, each has unique features that allow me to tell them apart. Our fingerprints, hair, and eyes are all different from those of others.

God intentionally paired you with suitable adults to become your parents, and you were birthed into existence through this intentional connection. It is my job and the job of your parents and mentors to help you discover your life's purpose. It is never too early to think about who you aspire to be. We are getting older, and we need you to step forward and continue the principles and lessons we have instilled in you. Our minds lose the ability to process information quickly like yours, and age will eventually limit our physical abilities. Therefore, you are vitally important to us and society.

The more you think about your destiny, the sooner you can move toward pursuing your dreams and fulfilling your purpose. Had someone talked to me about understanding my purpose at your age, I am confident I would be much further. I would have better understood the person I was meant to become. Knowing myself better would have brought me closer to my goals, and I would have been able to make better decisions to achieve them.

Now, let us discuss hobbies and interests. Do you have a favorite sport? Do you like math, science, or public speaking? What about music, or are you good at cooking or styling hair? It would be helpful to explore some of these options to identify your areas of giftedness. Identifying your talents will provide a sense of direction in what to pursue. Think about your favorite athlete, artist, comedian, or influencer. They use their gift to impact others; the world is their stage. Parents, teachers, coaches, and mentors serve as resources to nurture those talents. To achieve excellence, you must put in the hard work and dedicate time and effort if you desire to be the best in that field.

There is no urgency for you to figure everything out tomorrow. Instead, I aim to stimulate your mind to think about your future. Opportunities that can influence our decision-making will arise. Focusing on your purpose helps you remain dedicated to what you should be doing. A great future awaits you, and understanding your purpose is another key to unlocking your destiny.

Chapter 2: What Are Worth and Self-Validation?

Let us define the words worth and self-validation. Worth is "having something of value or desiring something useful." I view self-validation as the thoughts we believe to be true and acceptable about ourselves. The opinions that we consider to be important concerning ourselves. When you do not know your worth, the opinions of others can easily influence your decision-making.

Recognizing your worth and practicing self-validation is essential for building character. There are times when we look for others to validate who we are. We desire to join a particular social club or seek friendships with the popular kids in school for recognition. However, when you truly learn your worth, you lose the physical and emotional need for others to validate you. Honestly, the popular kids and those in your circle also seek validation. We have discussed that you are unique, which alone says a lot about you. God's creations are perfect; therefore, you are as well.

Worth also affects your self-esteem, and self-esteem can play a significant role in the decisions you make. Low self-esteem may lead you to succumb to social pressures by engaging in acts you would not do. These choices can be harmful and may not align with your values and beliefs. We will discuss these pressures in depth in our next chapter. Be confident in who you are because even the most beautiful and successful women have at least one insecurity. There is an area in their life where they lack confidence.

Bullies are an example of someone who will attempt to affect your self-esteem. They are cruel and thrive on the fear of others to cover up their flaws. They present an illusion of perfection but are far from that reality. Do not allow their thoughts or actions to undermine your confidence. They have encountered a negative experience that has influenced their unwanted behavior toward others. They, too, need a mentor or someone trustworthy to guide them.

I cannot stress the importance of knowing your worth and having self-confidence, especially regarding dating. This applies whether you have the support of your parents or are involved with someone without their knowledge. Understanding your value is a "must" if you desire to have a relationship with another person. I secretly dated because it would have been a definite "no" had I asked my mom. I had no idea what I was doing, and I relied on some friends to assist me as they attempted to do the same. Yep, they were clueless as well.

Picture yourself and a friend at the beach; you cannot swim. Curiosity encourages the two of you to venture into deeper waters; before you know it, you are far from shore. You rely on your friend for support, only to recognize she cannot swim either. Both of you find yourselves in a challenging situation, experiencing panic while figuring out what to do. Wishing you had remained close to shore, fear sets in as you wonder what is swimming beneath you. Finally, desperation signals the both of you to cry out for help. Thankfully, someone is around to rescue you in your moment of duress.

Dating is filled with uncertainties, and there are many aspects of a relationship you need help understanding. It seems like a great idea because someone told you that you were pretty. Your heart races and your emotions run high. However, the break-up occurs shortly after, and you begin to feel the opposite effect of those same emotions. Outwardly, you may seem unaffected as you move on to the next one, but deep down lies a lingering feeling of rejection. Maintaining your confidence can be challenging, but do not allow the situation to affect your self-esteem. Know from within that you are "good enough"; unfortunately, that person was not the right one to see that. When this happens, stay positive and wait to date again when you are emotionally stable. As you mature, in time, you will be able to experience a blossoming, authentic relationship the way God intended.

If I had waited to date, I could have also prevented some of these hard-knock lessons. I had a false belief about what love was. I was looking for an everlasting feeling from someone who did not understand the definition of love. The next time someone professes that you have their heart and declares their love for you, ask them what love means to them. I assure you they need to learn what the word truly means. They also need proper teaching of its meaning and significance. Take the time to enjoy being a teenager while discovering yourself. Talk about this topic with someone older and responsible enough to tell you the truth. Knowledge, understanding, and waiting are three words I would like you to remember concerning this subject.

Love is more than a feeling or a friendly gesture. The decision to love another person is a choice, a serious commitment. Consider your relationship with your parents. Do you stop loving them when you are angry with them? Absolutely not! The temporary feelings of anger fade, and you eventually forget about the situation that caused the disagreement. It is easy to forget and forgive them because your parents have consistently shown their love and loyalty through unwavering commitment. You trust in their dependability, knowing that they will always be there for you.

Do not allow your emotions to affect your ability to love. Instead, take a moment to clear your thoughts and think through the issue you are facing. Taking this time to assess the situation will help you to use good judgment. The goal is to have positive personal relationships and interactions with others. Learn to love yourself first before expressing it to someone in a relationship. I want you to share the gift of love with someone who understands its meaning and is willing to do what it takes to be a part of the relationship. Promise yourself to wait for love at this level and not rush it prematurely.

Taking this time to discover your internal qualities will enable you to ask someone else what unique attributes they have. If the person you are interested in is unsure of their qualities, evaluate the situation to see if the relationship is worth pursuing. Do not carry the burden of the relationship simply because it is what you desire. A healthy relationship is an equally shared partnership.

I am not only speaking about boys. I am referring to anyone you meet who desires friendship, and you want to be in their personal space to learn more about them. I have two friends who have been my best friends for over thirty years. My deep connection with them as best friends is not solely based on a feeling. While I genuinely care for them, my commitment to being their friend is a conscious choice. I am dedicated to them regardless of the circumstances.

Here are several attributes from God's word about love that guide us in keeping our commitments:

- ❖ "Love is patient, and love is kind."
- ❖ "It bears all things, believes all things, hopes for all things, and is always patient."
- ❖ "Love is not self-serving, jealous, boastful, or rude."
- ❖ "Love never ends."

Acquire Knowledge

Now, let us turn our attention to briefly discuss an internal quality: knowledge. Knowledge is a fundamental building block to uncovering your potential. Gaining knowledge is more important than focusing on your outer appearance. Women must have good grooming standards. However, let us also concentrate on passing our high school competency test or receiving a high score on our college entrance exams. Even if you decide to attend a trade school, which is also a great option, applying what you have learned from your educational experiences is still required. The gift of knowledge, another important key, is far more valuable than having expensive make-up and trendy clothing. We, as women, should aspire to have beauty and brains. Balancing both aspects creates an appealing charm that draws others to us.

Consider the value of a penny compared to a high-quality ruby. While we understand which one is more valuable, the real question is, how do you perceive yourself in this comparison? Do you see yourself as merely worth the penny, or can you recognize yourself as a rare find? The radiance of your inner beauty attracts the right one to you.

In my teenage years, I often thought about my forthcoming wedding day in hopes of receiving a beautiful engagement ring. Sharing such a gift from the right person at the right stage of your life is crucial. Maturity and purpose serve as a measurement of knowing if you both are ready. Seeking proper counsel ensures you both gain a thorough understanding of the duties and responsibilities of marriage. Marriage marks a beautiful beginning for your future, especially when you have taken the time to understand your value and purpose.

There is much information to process within this chapter, and I want you to reflect on the topics we have discussed. They are all vital tools for personal growth. Knowing your worth, gaining knowledge, and defining love all contribute to our collection of keys as we continue our journey of discovery. Consider this teaching as another opportunity to secure more keys that will shape your future.

Chapter 3: Overcoming Social Pressures

What is peer pressure? Peer pressure is the influence of others in your age group who may persuade you to make certain decisions or act in the same manner as the group. In some situations, this influence can encourage you to compromise on what is right and honest. Submitting to peer pressure may hide your creativity, keeping your gifts and talents undiscovered. Be the one who defies the norm to follow the crowd. Instead, follow the guidance of your inner being, your spirit.

As a teen, you may experience peer pressure, especially when it comes to wearing the latest shoes and clothing. Fashion is significantly important to your generation. I pray you never witness or experience the cruelty of others who tear down someone else's self-esteem if they cannot afford to wear stylish clothing. Avoid these types of people; they can be toxic.

I admit that I, too, submitted to peer pressure at times, wanting to please my friends and the person I was dating. There are moments when I wish to go back and make better choices. The real question we should ask ourselves is whether we have the strength and boldness to be different. Will you stand firmly on your beliefs or yield to the pressure to conform and align yourself with your peers? The decision between these two choices should be much easier now that we have discussed the meanings of worth and purpose.

I challenge you to be a trendsetter rather than a follower. Set your own rules, and dress to reflect your uniqueness. Most clothing and accessories are easily accessible for purchase, but it does not necessarily mean we should wear them. As ladies, we should wear clothing that positively communicates who we are. What we wear can make a statement as strong as our words. Whatever we choose to wear will capture the attention of a particular audience. Others may form opinions about you based on what they see, even if those perceptions are inaccurate.

This concept does not just apply to clothing. Become a leader in the classroom or set a positive example for your younger siblings. Remember, someone is always observing your behavior. Demonstrating your skills and maturity could open great doors of opportunity for you, as others are willing to invest in your future based on your potential.

Choose friends who consistently make good decisions and strive to be a friend known for making good choices. Those whose focus is securing their future by gaining knowledge to educate themselves. I do not mean to sound harsh, but I want to emphasize the negative impact of using illegal substances and excessive drinking. These behaviors can affect your brain cells and impede your thinking ability. Let us avoid the decisions that might alter our true selves. That person is not the one God designed to do remarkable things in this big world He has created. She is an imposter that comes to deter you from your appointed destination.

Now, let us discuss technology and social platforms, which teens consider essential to socializing. "Oh, how your little world would end if someone took this leisure away from you." When used appropriately, both technology and social media can be excellent tools. Social media can be an effective platform to display your skills and abilities. It can also provide laughter and joy as others share funny moments. Use good judgment when using these tools as you share your private moments with the world and search for answers to some of your questions. Although some of your peers post inappropriate personal comments and pictures and receive "likes," it does not make it acceptable for you to do the same. Certain moments in life are private and should not be shared.

Some employers and colleges view your social media profiles to assess your behavior and values. For example, an employer may want to determine if you are the right fit to work for their company. Similarly, colleges or universities seek potential students who will uphold their prestigious reputation upon acceptance. Even your desire to become an entrepreneur or social influencer should encourage you to display exemplary character and morals. Inspire change with uplifting words and gestures that are meaningful and charismatic.

I need you to understand what I am passionately relaying. Once you expose your life to the world, it can be challenging to remove those moments, especially if they are negative. Unfortunately, hitting the delete button will not always ensure that what you have erased is not recoverable. Modern technology now enables these moments to become resurrected from the graveyard of deleted photos and messages. The moments you share and events you post should serve the purpose of promoting or uplifting you or someone else.

Most of us enjoy some form of entertainment, and it is wise to be mindful of what we expose our eyes and ears to. Television is a favorite leisure pastime for many people. Let me paint a scenario for you. Imagine turning the channel to watch your favorite show, tuning out your surroundings, and immersing yourself in the characters' lives on the screen. You eagerly await each unfolding moment as the drama escalates with heated words, plots of retaliation, and physical actions that violate another person's personal space. When those minutes are up, the moments linger in your mind as you pick up the phone to dial a friend to discuss what happened. You passionately discuss the heroes and the villains as you dissect the situations of what you just witnessed. Eventually, you snap back to the real world, discovering that your parents have been calling you to do something productive.

What we see and hear can influence the shaping of our character. These individuals have gained popularity and become role models. The lifestyle of money and fame has you desiring that same way of living. Let me share with you a wisdom principle: money should not define you as a person. Its purpose is to assist with fulfilling your life's purpose while enhancing your quality of life. Please do not allow the love money to control your character. Acquiring money does not guarantee happiness and self-fulfillment, and no one wants to befriend someone hostile and arrogant.

Allow me to pose a question to you. What would you like others to remember you for as you mature into adulthood and fulfill your responsibility of becoming a productive member of society? You could be the chemist who found a cure for her grandmother's cancer or dementia or the influencer who led their generation forward to reshape our world with messages of hope. Let your life's achievements speak for you. Strive to be an individual with diverse skills through attaining knowledge in your areas of interest.

On the contrary, some entertainers and television hosts serve as excellent role models. I admire a few, and maybe you will become one. If being an entertainer aligns with your purpose, then pursue it. Your actions and mindset are the only things that can hold you back from achieving greatness. I want to express to you that "I believe in you."

Our response to life's occurrences affects us significantly and can even impact our family. Every positive or negative decision will affect our existence. Please do not allow the pressure of people and things to dictate how you respond to a situation. As a young teenage woman, I can only imagine your challenges today. I am utterly speechless at times as I listen to the issues my teen nieces face while advising them on overcoming their opposition. Sometimes, they do not like my response but respect my wisdom. They know that I have their best interest at heart. I love them and will never damage their emotions or self-esteem.

Our world today differs from when your parents and I grew up. Still, I am confident we will be able to coach you through life's challenging circumstances. Life experiences tend to repeat themselves in each generation; remember, we also faced challenges associated with social pressures as teens. Even today, we as adults continue to experience social pressures. They do not leave as we enter adulthood. The decision-making process becomes more of a challenge, and time does not stop as you figure out what you need to do.

As stated in the previous chapter, having a healthy, trustful relationship with your parents or a reliable adult is beneficial. If you talk to them, you may discover they are interested in knowing what you are feeling and experiencing. In addition, you need a wise and strong support system if you are going to be successful. So, take some time to reflect on the lessons within the chapter. This topic is a critical learning key because it is a life experience that will accompany you as you age.

Chapter 4: Just Dream

-To Be or Not To Be-

As a kid, I would lie in bed and stare at the ceiling while my thoughts wandered to distant places that seemed impossible to visit. I would think about famous people and destinations I would like to see and visit. Both Paris and Michael Jackson have continuously topped my list of interests. Yet, at least one of those dreams is still in reach as it remains on my bucket list.

It took my mind at least an hour to unwind before I could drift off to sleep. During that time, I often thought about the next school day, contemplating everything from my outfit to the steps leading to my high school graduation. I was eager to graduate and step into the real world. I sometimes ask myself why I was so anxious to become an adult. As I reflect, those were some of the best moments of my life. My only responsibility was to attend school to prepare myself for the future. The technology that you enjoy today did not exist during my teenage years. School and church were my only social outlets, and I could not wait to see my friends again. Life was simple.

Even at this age, I still daydream if I sit quietly long enough. My thoughts constantly race, and I must slow down to process my ideas. It is important to channel your thoughts as you weigh which opportunities to pursue when inspiration seems to bloom like spring flowers. Dreaming is a vital part of life. It inspires confidence as you work to enhance who you will someday become.

Reflecting on my accomplishments, I can trace their beginnings to a dream. In my mind, I could see myself obtaining what I envisioned. I would translate those thoughts to paper to follow through with my plan and, ultimately, accomplish each goal. The cool thing about dreams is seeing them become a reality; this book is an example. Initially, I began sending daily motivational texts to my closest friends, and as I continued, I recognized the potential for a book. Now, I am having a conversation with you through its various sections. Writing this book is a gift that allows me to reach and inspire many young women I have yet to meet.

What is Vision?

We have been blessed not only with natural sight from God but also with the incredible power of thought and imagination. Those thoughts have the potential to become a reality. What if I told you that your life is a canvas, and whatever you envision is possible to achieve? The question is, how much time are you willing to invest in bringing your ideas to life? Imagine achieving success while pursuing a talent you love. Some may reply that you are still just a kid and want to enjoy your remaining freedom without thinking about the future. However, adulthood is just around the corner after your teenage years, leaving a brief time to prepare.

I fought back the tears when my nieces walked across the stage to receive their high school diplomas. The joy I would feel was overwhelming. It seemed only yesterday that I was changing their diapers and attending birthday parties. Now, they are young adults, ready to explore and pursue what they have envisioned becoming. Guess who is waiting to be there to continue being their mentor?

Whatever you envision and dream for yourself, ensure it serves a purpose. Start by asking the Heavenly Father in prayer to reveal your path, as each person's destiny is different. As you and your friends desire to share each other's vision, remember that we are each created to do something different. My friends and I have different talents, and I admire them all.

I have a friend who excels as a designer and decorator, showcasing her ability to decorate under pressure with results that seem like weeks of effort. Another friend is a business owner and manager. She is also a great singer. Her position requires her to be bold and firm, yet she shows compassion when needed. Her powerful voice can change the atmosphere in any room.

I also have a friend who is a nurse. She is highly knowledgeable in her skillset, and her passion for helping others is a gift that I also admire. One of my best friends is also in the mortgage industry and is very knowledgeable about buying a home. This chapter would be excessively long if I were to describe all the talents of my friends. We all love what we do and use our skills and talents to pursue our dreams. Being surrounded by others living their dreams encourages you to focus on what you need to accomplish.

Now that you understand the meaning of vision, let us create a vision board. It can consist of a board with an album of pictures or images and goals you want to attain. You can purchase an erasable board, make a canvas, use a planner, or do anything similar to write your goals. Whatever creative display you would like to use to help you stay focused on your dreams. My vision board allows me to see my future goals physically, and I put a completion checkmark when I finish each one. Eventually, I erase those completed and replace them with new goals I want to achieve. I periodically keep a mental note or view the finished product as motivation to finish the others.

A vision board is great for writing short- and long-term goals. Witnessing your dreams on display can be incredibly motivating. It will also give you something to work towards while sitting at home during the summer or on weekends in boredom. Invite your friends over, and you all can create your boards together. You will be amazed at the unique ideas each friend brings to the table.

Focusing on your goals fills your mind with positive thoughts, seals your lips from gossip and drama, and keeps your hands busy, steering clear of mischief. I know that sounds lame, but you have plenty of time to do other fun things. There are times to relax and enjoy life, and there are times to be serious and focused. Are you focused when taking your driver's exam or considering your friend's upcoming weekend party? That is one of the purposes of the adults in your life, to help you achieve balance.

Find a Mentor

Finding someone older you can entrust to share your life experiences is necessary. Everyone needs a mentor. This individual should be mature and responsible, model positive behavior, and have the ability to nurture personal or professional growth. Examples include a teacher, a relative, a spiritual leader, or a boss. I have learned the importance of having a mentor at each stage of life. No matter our intelligence level, there will always be some things that we can only understand to a certain extent.

As a teen, you may lack comfort sharing life experiences with your parents. It is not because your parents are "bad" parents, but you are unsure how they would react if you told them about certain situations. I can relate because I felt the same way about my mom. She was a great parent but strict, and I was afraid to ask her about some of my curiosities. However, I had a cool aunt. She was firm as well but very approachable and relatable. She would sometimes be the mediator between my mom and me when we could not agree. Occasionally, it worked; other times, we both walked away in disappointment. I treasure them and value their guidance and wisdom now that I am older.

I am fortunate to have both personal and professional mentors. One of my great friends is also my life coach. She has the gifts of wisdom and knowledge concerning life issues. When I need personal advice, I can call her. I can trust her to safeguard the information I share with her, and I know she will give me truthful feedback, whether I like it or not. Her sincerity and sense of humor add to the value I place on our relationship.

I also have a few professional mentors from previous jobs who were initially my bosses. I observed them to see how they managed situations and people. I watched their character and values. Over time, most of them have become my good friends. I can easily reach out to them and engage in casual conversations as we catch up on our life occurrences. Even today, they willingly offer personal and professional career advice when I need it. These moments allow me to reflect on the people who have helped mold me into the person I have become. I am overwhelmed with gratitude.

As you become the woman God intends you to be, opportunities to help others will arise. Sharing your newfound knowledge is a wise choice. Your impact on helping others will be shaped by your obedience and your willingness to listen, learn, and grow. I know this to be true observing my mother over the years, and now, her guidance has empowered me to successfully use my gifts to mentor others.

My mom is my most influential mentor. Her words, actions, and stare all make a strong statement that compels you to be attentive. She teaches by example, showing love to everyone, even strangers. She brings family and friends together for fellowship with her gift of cooking. On Sundays, there is never a dull moment at "BigMa's" house. Time and wisdom have guided her in using her gifts to influence others positively.

Although I chose to address the importance of dreaming in the final chapter, it is one of your most vital keys. Take the time to dream big and plan out your next steps to achieve extraordinary things. Let me remind you of that empty canvas and all the possibilities. Get excited about the woman you are becoming. Life is preparing you for that center-stage moment. Confidence and preparedness will help you succeed when that time comes. The possibilities are endless! Just imagine!

Wrap Up…

On this journey, we have discovered the importance of protecting the keys that shape who we are. Your teen years should be exciting, purposeful, and curious for knowledge. As your parents and mentors, we anticipate you will have pertinent questions that will cultivate your growth process. Before ending this journey, let us highlight some key points with a brief recap.

We began by using our master key to have an open mind. It is vital to have an open mindset to grasp the concepts and life lessons discussed. When we keep an open mind, we gain the confidence to chase after the opportunities awaiting us. Using the second key, we explored the meanings of destiny and purpose, two vital words during the discovery process. Understanding your purpose serves as motivation to reveal your gifts and talents.

The third key, Worth, is equally important. Knowing our inner values helps us accept and embrace the truths we discover. The fourth key, "love," has a profound impact on our emotions and enables us to open our hearts. Knowing the true meaning of the word "love" allows us to determine when and how to express it. Let love be a guiding principle as you interact with those around you.

The next key highlights the significance of acquiring knowledge. Pursuing knowledge and wisdom helps us to comprehend and apply the lessons learned from education and life experiences as we mature. We can overcome life's challenges, including social pressures, with knowledge and understanding. Remember, social influences impact our decision-making process and reveal our morals and character. Let us ensure that our character reflects integrity. When mastered, we permit ourselves to set our own rules and defy society's definition of success.

Our final key unlocked the realm of dreams, exposing a world of limitless possibilities. Dreaming ignites our imagination, encouraging us to explore our goals. Take the opportunity to write what you want to accomplish as you think about your dreams. Remember, dreaming provides the vision to see what you aim to achieve.

Now that you thoroughly understand the topics covered in these chapters, take a moment to consider how these concepts can help you pursue your goals. Consider adding them to your vision board as a reminder of your aspirations. Seek God's guidance through prayer on how to achieve your goals and provide solutions to your daily challenges. If you need assistance, this is another opportunity to ask for help from a parent or mentor. Do your best to apply these subject matters effectively.

As you navigate life's journey, you will discover many keys. Hopefully, the discussion on these primary keys has sparked your curiosity to explore further opportunities for learning and growth. I foresee nothing but greatness in your future. If no one has acknowledged the greatness within you, allow me to be the first to confidently affirm it. The first requirement is for you to believe in yourself. Secondly, you must believe that anything is possible concerning your purpose.

The Master key holds the power to unlock the six remaining keys: the Purpose Key, the Key of Worth, the Key to Knowledge, the Love Key, the Key to Conquer, and the Dream Key. All of these keys you possess complement and build upon each other. Please do not allow people and circumstances to seize control of them, as it may result in relinquishing control of your destiny. Remembering this wisdom nugget: "Protecting my keys equals protecting my identity."

Keys are only useful once the owner decides to use them. You alone can unlock doors that shape the outcome of your future. No human has the authority to close a door that God has opened. Challenges of roadblocks may occur, but remain persistent, and you will reach your destination at the appointed time. Discovering your purpose lies within you, with God being the ultimate source of the discovery. Take a moment to look within, and trust that with God's help, you will find your way. The world is watching and awaiting your response. Perhaps one day, I will have the privilege of learning from you.

Signing off for now,

Your mentor.

Here are a few questions to consider, and I encourage you to provide honest answers. Answering these questions can enable you to become the best version of yourself!

"Often Imitated, Never Duplicated!"

- ❖ What do I like about me in general?
- ❖ What do I like about my physical appearance (eyes, hair, face, body)?
- ❖ What does my character say about me?
- ❖ What do I have that no one else has, nor can they take away?

Seven Key Takeaways

- ❖ "Mind your Mind"- The mind is the master key to unlocking destiny!
- ❖ Identity- Protecting my keys equals protecting my identity
- ❖ Trending- Set the trend instead of just being apart!
- ❖ Love- What it is versus what it is not!
- ❖ Discovery and pursuit will lead me to greatness!
- ❖ The more I know, the more I grow!
- ❖ Dreaming ignites the vision to see my future!

References

MacArthur, J. F., Jr. (2008a). *Jacob and Egypt: The Sovereignty of God.* Thomas Nelson.

Waters, M. (2014). *Ancient Persia: A Concise History of the Achaemenid Empire, 550–330 BCE.* Cambridge University Press.

Hindson, & Ice. (2017). *Charting the Bible Chronologically: A Visual Guide to God's Unfolding Plan.* Harvest House Publishers.

Brand, C., Mitchell, E., Holman Reference Editorial Staff, & Staff, H. R. E. (2015). *Holman Illustrated Bible Dictionary.* Van Haren Publishing.

Nelson, T., & MacArthur, J. F. (2013). *The NASB, MacArthur Study Bible, Hardcover: Holy Bible, New American Standard Bible* (Updated ed.). Thomas Nelson.

McSpadden, K. (2015, May 14). You Now Have a Shorter Attention Span Than a Goldfish. *Time.* Retrieved March 27, 2022, from https://time.com/3858309/attention-spans-goldfish/

permission. Holman Christian Standard Bible®, Holman CSB® and HCSB® are federally registered trademarks of Holman Bible Publishers.

Barnes, Atavia, S (2017). The Hurt That Helped Heart: Anatomy and Function (clevelandclinic.org)

"Opposition," *Merriam-Webster.com Dictionary*, https://www.merriam-webster.com/dictionary/opposition. Accessed 8/29/2022.

"Opportunity," *Merriam-Webster.com Dictionary*, https://www.merriam-webster.com/dictionary/opportunity. Accessed 8/29/2022.

OpenAI. "GPT-3.5-based ChatGPT." OpenAI, www.openai.com. Accessed January 2024.

App.grammarly.com

Arapovic, Benis. American football players are ready to start on field at night. Digital image. www.shutterstock.com

Images were taken from Microsoft ® Word for Microsoft 365 MSO (Version 2207)